Śrī Bhakti Rakṣaka Bhajana Mādhurī

Śrī Śrī Guru-Gaurāṅga-Gāndharvā-Govinda-Sundarajīu-Pāda-Padmānām Jayastu

Śrī Bhakti Rakṣaka Bhajana Mādhurī

A Glimpse into the Heart
of Srila Guru Maharaja

by Bhakti Nandan Swami

The conclusion of Srila Guru Maharaja's bhajan
in the form of devotional songs in his last days

MANDALA
publishing group

Singapore San Francisco Mumbai

Mandala Publishing Group

1585-A Folsom Street
San Francisco California
USA 94103
Tel : 415.621. 2336 Fax : 415.626.1063

239C Joo Chiat Road
SINGAPORE, 427496
Tel: 65. 342. 3117 Fax: 65. 342. 3115

Centerpoint Bldg.
World Trade Center
Center 1, 30th floor
Cuffe Parade, Mumbai
INDIA, 400005
Fax: 91. 22. 218. 8175

Email: mandala@mandala.org
url: www.mandala.org

ISBN:1886069-01-8
Printed in China through Palace Press International, San Francisco

CONTENTS

DEDICATION

This book is dedicated to all the loving followers of Śrīla Guru Mahārāja and to all other devotees who are deeply fond of honoring and appreciating a pure Vaiṣṇava.

ACKNOWLEDGEMENTS

The translations from *Brahma-saṁhitā* presented in Chapter Four are by His Divine Grace Śrīla Bhaktisiddhānta Saraswatī Goswāmī Prabhupāda.

My special thanks and gratitude to Swātī Mā, without whom this book would not have easily come to light. An uncut gemstone was placed before her, and by her valuable suggestions and editing of the manuscript, she gave it shape and form. My special thanks and regard go to her good husband Mādhurya-līla Prabhu also, for his continuous affectionate support and valuable assistance.

Final English Editing: Śrīpada Sajjana Swāmī
Editorial Assistance: Śrīmatī Kamala Prīyā devī dāsī
Design & Layout: Jai Gopāl dās
Contributors: Śrī Rāmatanuja dās Adhīkārī and Śrīmatī Gopinī devī dāsī
Special Thanks to Śrī Rāmadās dās and Mandala Media

PREFACE

The inner subjective world of divine realization is infinitely charming and attractive. It is most illuminating and beautifully mysterious. It is full of eternal truth, auspiciousness and ecstasy, and its nature is oneness in diversity.

Being a member of that transcendental world, a pure devotee has different wonderful experiences in relation to the Lord of that world, who is his worshipable beloved, the Personality of Godhead, Kṛṣṇa. These experiences reveal the nectarean relationship between the Lord and His devotee which sometimes manifests in the sheer delight of union, the sweet sadness of separation, and other variegated devotional mellows. A pure devotee adores these invaluable experiences with all his heart. Here, then, is a glimpse of such moments from the life of an exclusively devoted servitor of the Supreme Lord, Śrīmad Bhakti Rakṣaka Śrīdhara Deva Goswāmī Mahārāja.

PRAṆĀMA-MAṆTRA

tuṅga-nitya-siddha-kṛṣṇa-bhāva-bhakti-rakṣakaṁ
śrīdharaṁ subhakti-sindhu śuddha-bhakta-vanditam
kṛṣṇa-rādhikā-sukhābdhi-gaura-bhakti-sundaraṁ
śrīdharaṁ bhajāmi bhakti-rakṣakaṁ cira-prabhum

With his heart filled with ecstatic love of Gaura,
he is the magnificent ocean of sweet devotion
to *Śrī Rādhikā* and *Kṛṣṇa*. Pure devotees fondly glorify him
as the caretaker and guardian of devotion.
I perpetually worship him, my beloved divine master,
Śrīmad Bhakti Rakṣaka Śrīdhara Deva Goswāmī, with full devotion.

śrī-sarasvatī-priyeṣṭa-sevanaṁ suvigrahaṁ
śrī-svarūpa-rāya-rūpa-rāga-raśmi-sundaram
rādhikā-sudivya-bhāva-rañjitaṁ priyaṁ vadhūṁ
śrīdharaṁ bhajāmi bhakti-rakṣakaṁ cira-prabhum

He is the embodiment of confidential service to
Śrīla Saraswatī Ṭhākura and is decorated with the radiance of
rāga-bhakti emanating from his *guru-varga* headed by
Śrī Svarūpa Dāmodara, Rāya Rāmānanda, and *Śrīla Rūpa Goswāmī.*
In his *siddha-rūpa* he is a damsel of *Vraja* imbued with
superexcellent devotion to *Śrī Rādhikā.*
I perpetually worship him, my beloved divine master,
Śrīmad Bhakti Rakṣaka Śrīdhara Deva Goswāmī, with full devotion.

Śrīmad Bhakti Rakṣaka Śrīdhara Deva Goswāmī Mahārāja

Prabhupāda Śrīla Bhakti Siddhānta Sarasvatī Ṭhākura

Śrīla Saccidānanda Bhaktivinode Ṭhākura

Śrī Śrī Guru-Gaurāṇga-Gandhārvvā Govindasundarajiu

Śrīmad Bhakti Rakṣaka Śrīdhara-Deva Goswāmī Mahārāja

Śrī Śrī Rādhā Kṛṣṇa

INTRODUCTION

One day in the year 1996 while working on Śrīla Guru Mahārāja's biography, I was listening to some of the beautiful verses spontaneously recited by him in devotional absorption during the last year of his life. The vivid memory of his priceless association during those special moments once again deeply touched my heart with unforgettable sweetness and charm.

The divine essence of these sacred verses as tasted by Śrīla Guru Mahārāja is known by all pure devotees throughout the ages and remains eternally ever available in this world as the summum bonum of life. Despite my own inadequate qualification to properly deal with such an exalted subject matter I felt a special inspiration to somehow share this treasure with his devotees.

This book contains some of the devotional *bhajans* and selected verses uttered by Śrīla Guru Mahārāja as he was absorbed in his personal devotional mood. He relished these verses mostly in a secluded way with tears of deep emotion as he became imbued with their *bhāva* throughout his existence.

During 1987-88 it became apparent that Śrīla Guru Mahārāja considered his spiritual task accomplished and was preparing to withdraw his manifest presence from this earthly plane to unite with the Divine Couple in Their *nitya-līlā*. He was most eagerly looking forward to this with divine 'homesickness,' and therefore the feelings of his utterances are imbued with the transcendental sweet pain of separation, mystic loneliness, humility, and hankering for perfection.

These songs were mostly recorded during twilight or dark evenings. He used to sit on his simple easy chair on the southern verandah or on the bed outside his room facing the east. At other times he would sit on the roof of the *nāṭya mandir* before his Lord's temple, which was often mystically illuminated by the moon and stars in the sky. He would experience the beautiful breeze from Mother Gaṅgā blowing through the flowers and trees of Śrī Caitanya Sāraswata Maṭh, which would cool and soothe him at these moments.

His recitations are all basically of a personal subjective nature—like talking or singing to himself. He was not doing it to be listened to by others, but only to relate to his beloved Lord with intimate internal absorption. Thus many of these recitations, not clearly pronounced, were uttered for his own hearing as he entered into them and tasted their deep esoteric moods of ecstasy from the *mahābhāgavata* platform. Such moods of an *uttama adhikārī* are fathomless and mysterious and are not always easily comprehended. But to have some glimpse into them is certainly a great fortune in life.

Following the principle that sometimes one may exceptionally steal the grace of Śrī Gurudeva this humble servitor could not check himself from capturing these memories of Śrīla Guru Mahārāja, who was often not even aware that I was recording him. It appeared that Śrīla Guru Mahārāja was receiving divine grace descending upon him and that potency of devotion permeated the entire atmosphere around him. I was therefore inspired to save some of those special moments of his divine experience for the devotees who have deep love for him and can truly taste and adore such valuable wealth in their heart.

Although Śrīla Guru Mahārāja recited these verses spontaneously without following any apparent order, for the sake of clearer understanding of the readers, the flow of his devotional moods have been presented here as far as possible according to *tattva*. They begin with describing Śrīla Guru Mahārāja's relationship with Śrī Nityānanda Prabhu, the representation of supreme *guru-tattva*, and the all-merciful *premāvatāra* Śrī

Caitanya Mahāprabhu, progressing to his love and appreciation of Śrī Nāma Prabhu, the divine Holy Name. The following chapter addresses Śrīla Guru Mahārāja's devotion to the Personality of Godhead Śrī Kṛṣṇa and His beautiful attributes, progressing to the description of Śrī Rādhikā, the all-encompassing Divine Mistress of his life. The final chapter concludes with Śrīla Guru Mahārāja's *mañjarī sādhanā,* praying to the lotus feet of the divine damsels of Vraja to attain Śrī Rādhā-*dāsyam,* the ultimate goal of his life, under the shelter of Śrī Rūpa Mañjarī.

There are many other verses recited by Śrīla Guru Mahārāja that could not be recorded because of his uncalculative, sudden, spontaneous nature, and also out of respect for his secluded personal mood. Where it seemed necessary, the texts of songs *not* recorded are included to help create a deeper import into his mood. The explanations and elaborations of the songs and verses throughout this book are based on tapes and Śrīla Guru Mahārāja's personal instruction to me. Offering respectful obeisances to the holy lotus feet of Śrīla Guru Mahārāja, this humble servitor prays for his divine grace, which can bring a wonderful transcendental fortune to one's life.

It is our sincere wish that the readers of this collection of memories of Śrīla Guru Mahārāja receive his merciful benediction in their lives and attain a glimpse into the *bhajan* of an exalted devotee.

Chapter One

NITYĀNANDA-TATTVA

Śrīla Guru Mahārāja looked upon Śrī Nityānanda Prabhu as a great and favorite source of inspiration in his life whom he adored as an exalted *avadhuta* absorbed in the esoteric mellows of devotion. He accepted Him as the personified love of Śrīmān Mahāprabhu and the nondifferent manifestation of Baladeva Prabhu who in *mādhurya rasa* appears in Śrīmatī Rādhārānī's camp of intimate associates as Anaṅga Mañjarī, one of the topmost servitors of the Divine Couple.

As the special expansion of the supreme *guru-tattva,* Nityānanda Prabhu ever remained as an inseparable part of Śrīla Guru Mahārāja's *bhajan* life. Nityānanda Prabhu's affection as the most magnanimous distributor of Gaura-*prema,* regardless of caste or creed, as well as His ecstatic upsurge of divine love for both Śrīmān Mahāprabhu and The Divine Couple, deeply attracted Śrīla Guru Mahārāja's heart. In his last days Śrīla Guru Mahārāja loved to deeply utter "*Dayāl Nitāi*! *Dayāl Nitāi*!" with great devotional conviction and tearful eyes. He prayed for the grace of Nityānanda Prabhu with so much heartfelt absorption that his devotees and admirers took this as a new holy *maṇtra* in their lives.

Remembering the grace of Nityānanda Prabhu, Śrīla Guru Mahārāja would often relish with appreciation the moods of his *guru-varga* and other *mahājana padāvalī* such as *Nitāi guṇamaṇi āmār, Nitāi jīvan āmār, Śrī Nityānandāṣṭakam,* and others. Explaining some of his favorite verses and songs, he described Nityānanda Prabhu's great compassion and prideless approach for blessing everyone with the ambrosial gift of Gaura-*prema*, unifying in His character the extraordinary nobility and humility that fully embody Śrīmān Mahāprabhu's principle of *tṛṇādapi sunīcena*.

bhaja gaurāṅga kaha gaurāṅga laha gaurāṅgera nāma re
ye janā gaurāṅga bhaje sei haya āmār prāṇa re

Śrīmān Nityānanda Prabhu mercifully calls out: "Please always worship Gaurāṅga, speak about Him, and take His Holy Name with all devotion. One who adores My beloved master Gaurāṅga is as dear to Me as My own life."

yenā bhaje tāre bale dante tṛṇa dhari
āmāre kiniyā laha bala gaura-hari
eta bali nityānanda bhūme gaḍi yāya
sonāra parvata yena dhūlāya loṭāya

The compassionate Nityānanda Prabhu most humbly approached those who did not feel any loving appreciation for Śrī Gaurāṅga due to their false pride and hardheartedness. So as not to hurt their pride, He took a few blades of grass between His teeth as a token of humility and appealed to them, saying, "O dear friend, try to understand that your own highest good is Gaurahari. You can attain the greatest fortune of your life if you connect to Him with love and devotion. Please take His Holy Name, even if only once, and chant it from the core of your heart. With devotional faith speak about His glories and share your relish with other devotees. Sincerely pray for His grace, for you will surely receive great spiritual benefit. I am your most well-wishing friend. If you can please take my advice and act accordingly, then you can own Me forever." Imploring in such a way, Śrī Nityānanda's heart melted in spiritual compassion. Incited by that deep emotional ecstasy He became so tender before those proud people that He invalidated all their pride. In noble humility He began to roll on the ground before them. As His form became decorated with the dust of the earth, the devotees around Him beheld with tearful eyes the extraordinary manifestation of the causeless mercy of Prabhu Nityānanda. They marveled at how their divine *guru-tattva* could sacrifice His honor and exalted position, coming down to the dust of the earth with such compassionate humility."

—Locana dāsa Ṭhākura

preme matta nityānanda kṛpā-avatāra
uttama adhama kichu nā kare vicāra
ye āge paḍaye tāre karaye nistāra
ataeva nistārilā mo-hena durācāra
(ataeva mo adhame karilena pāra)

"Lord Nityānanda, who is always intoxicated by divine love, is the great savior of destitute *jīvas* and the magnanimous incarnation of divine mercy. His benevolent nature does not discriminate between high and low or qualified and unqualified. He simply delivers from material existence anyone who comes before Him and falls at His lotus feet surrendering themselves to Him with all sincerity. Therefore He also mercifully delivered me, who am so fallen and unqualified."

—Kṛṣṇadāsa Kavirāja, *Śrī Caitanya-caritāmṛta, Ādi* 5.208-209

nitāi-pada-kamala koṭī-candra-suśītala
ye chāyāya jagata juḍāya

hena nitāi vine bhāi rādhā-kṛṣṇa pāite nāi
dṛḍha kari' dhara nitāir pāya

se sambandha nāhi yāra bṛthā janma gela tāra
sei paśu baḍa durācāra
nitāi nā balila mukhe majila saṁsāra-sukhe
vidyā-kule ki karibe tāra

ahaṅkāre matta haiyā nitāi-pada pāsariyā
asatyere satya kari māni
nitāiyera karuṇā habe vraje rādhā-kṛṣṇa pābe
dhara nitāi-caraṇa du'khāni

nitāiyer-caraṇa satya tānhāra sevaka nitya
nitāi-pada sadā kara āśa
narottama baḍa dukhī nitāi more kara sukhī
rākha rāṅgā-caraṇera pāśa

"The lotus feet of Prabhu Nityānanda are most pleasing, like the combined calming radiance of millions of moons. By receiving the cooling shade of His transcendental shelter, the whole universe, scorched by the heat of material existence, can be fully relieved and soothed. O dear brothers, without the grace of such a magnanimous personality as Prabhu Nityānanda, it is very difficult to attain divine loving service to Śrī Rādhā and Kṛṣṇa in the groves of Vṛndāvana. Therefore firmly take shelter of His lotus feet with all sincere respect and love so that you may reach that nectarean goal.

"A person who has not strived to receive any blessed connection with Nityānanda Prabhu or His invaluable wealth, which is ecstatic love of Godhead, becomes materially entangled, and his intelligence gets misused for animal propensities. Compared to the higher life of divine taste, such a life is considered wasted. Those who do not know the great fortune of taking the name of Nityānanda as well as those who deliberately ignore Him, become more and more intoxicated and addicted to mundane happiness.

"Without a connection to the eternal blissful nature of Nityānanda Prabhu, what real protection can the satisfaction of mundane education or a boast of heritage give in this insecure mortal world?

"Being maddened and bewildered by false pride, such persons forget their eternal relationship with Nityānanda and do not attain the great solace of His lotus feet; they thus accept illusion as reality.

"My friends, if Nityānanda Prabhu gives you mercy, only then can you attain the service of Rādhā-Kṛṣṇa, the Divine Couple of Vraja; therefore firmly embrace His lotus feet and beg Him for His grace. Please know that the shelter of the lotus feet of Nityānanda Prabhu are eternally true and the giver of all transcendental fulfillment.

"One who engages in the loving service of Nityānanda with perfection is understood to have attained that plane of eternal truth and fulfillment. Therefore always pray and hope for the shelter of Śri Nityānanda Prabhu's lotus feet. Narottama says, 'O merciful Prabhu Nitāi, I find myself unsatisfied because I have an endless hankering for more of the taste of Your nectarean grace. So please satisfy this need of mine and make me very happy by keeping me close to Your lotus feet, which are ever imbued with the hue of divine ecstasy.'"

—Narottama dāsa Ṭhākura, *Prārthanā*

Śrīla Guru Mahārāja entered deeply into the realization of the beautiful attributes and distinct characteristics of the personality of Śrī Nityānanda Prabhu. Being so captivated by Nityānanda Avadhuta's exalted devotion, Śrīla Guru Mahārāja saw Him as an intimate devotee and as nondifferent from Śrīmān Mahāprabhu and the Divine Couple. Feeling special inspiration, Śrīla Guru Mahārāja composed a beautiful *stotram* known as *Nityānanda-dvādaśakam*. These are the concluding words of his deep prayer of supplication to the lotus feet of Nityānanda Prabhu:

śrī-rādhā kṛṣṇa-līlā rasa-madhura-sudhāsvāda-śuddhaika-mūrtau
gaure śraddhāṁ dṛḍhāṁ bho prabhu-parikara-samrāṭ prayacchādhame'smin
ullaṅghyāṅghriṁ hi yasyākhila-bhajana-kathā svapnavac-caiva mithyā
śrī-nityānanda-candraṁ patita-śaraṇadaṁ gauradaṁ taṁ bhaje'ham

"O Nityānanda Prabhu, emperor amidst the dear associates of Śrīmān Mahāprabhu, please bless this fallen soul with resolute faith and devotion to Śrī Gaurāṅga. Lord Gaurāṅga's personality exclusively embodies the sweet nectar relished deep within the devotional mellows of Śrī Śrī Rādhā-Kṛṣṇa's pastimes. If Your lotus feet are deliberately overlooked, then all so-called devotional prayers and worship of Gaurāṅga and the Divine Couple become false like a dream; but anyone who is devoted to Your holy feet can eventually attain all divine success. I worship You, O Nityānanda Prabhu. Your mercy is my great hope. Please embrace me in the shelter of Your lotus feet and engage me in the service of Śrī Gaurāṅga."

Chapter Two

GAURA-TATTVA

Śrī Gaurāṅga, the embodiment of divine ecstatic love of Kṛṣṇa, became the ideal and most beloved worshipable object of Śrīla Guru Mahārāja's *bhajan* life. In his early adult life Śrīla Guru Mahārāja received some special impetus from the divine plane of his inner world to discover more about the Supreme Absolute Truth and he could not but respond to it with all his heart. He thus began intensely seeking that higher connection with great eagerness, accepting it as the utmost necessity of his life. During that time he discovered Śrī Gaurāṅga and His unparalleled gift of Kṛṣṇa-*prema,* and realized that it was everything he had been searching for.

The more deeply he entered into the domain of Gaura-*tattva,* the more he felt intense love and devotion for this most magnanimous *premāvatāra,* the incarnation of ecstatic divine love. Like other pure devotees, he accepted full shelter of Gaurāṅga, recognizing Him as nondifferent from Śrī Rādhā-Kṛṣṇa, the supreme divine truth of all blissful perfection. The cherished intimate association of his *gurudeva* Śrīla Saraswatī Ṭhākura further promoted his devotion and appreciation of Mahāprabhu. Śrīla Guru Mahārāja felt special gratitude towards him and other stalwart Gaura-*bhaktas* who glorified Śrī Gaurāṅga through their heartfelt songs and compositions. He would remain absorbed in relishing the nectarean moods of such songs as *Gorā pahun, Gaurāṅga bolite habe, Hā hā mora gaura kiśora, Avatāra sāra, Dhāola nadīyā loka, Nīrada nayane, Kalau yaṁ vidvāṁsaḥ, Sadopāsyaḥ śrīmān,* and *Harir dṛṣṭvā goṣṭhe*, as well as verses such as *Anarpita-carīṁ cirāt, Rādhā kṛṣṇa praṇaya, Śrī rādhāyā praṇaya mahimā, Sañcārya rāmānanda, Heloddhūlita khedayā*, and others. Some others are as follows:

e mana gaurāṅga vinu nāhi ār
hena avatāra habe ki hayeche
hena prema paracār
śiva viriñcira vāñchita ye dhana
jagate phelila ḍhāli
kāṅgāle pāiye khāila nāciye
bājāiye karatāli
nāciyā gāhiyā khola karatāle
dhāiyā mātiyā phire
tarāsa pāiye śamaṇa kiṅkara
kabāṭa hānila dvāre
e tina bhuvana ānande bharila
uṭhila maṅgala śora
kahe premānande ehena gaurāṅge
rati nā janmila mora

"O mind, please listen. You have nothing else to be attached to except Śrī Gaurāṅga. Never in the past nor in the future will there be such a benevolent incarnation who has presented the matchless divine love-ecstasy of God so generously. He poured into this world that ambrosial wealth which is ever cherished and hankered for even by powerful and great personalities like Śiva and Viriñci (Brahmā). By His merciful grant even the most common destitute persons were blessed with the chance to imbibe that nectar with great delight. Overwhelmed by spiritual ecstasy, they began to sing the glory of the Lord and dance accompanied by the concert of rhythmic drums and sweet *karatālas*. Frightened by the power of such holy *saṅkīrtana*, the inauspicious atheists who were slaves to their mortal egos ran away and hid in locked rooms to protect themselves from its purifying effect. All three worlds of existence (*svarga, martya,* and *pātāla*) became blessed by receiving transcendental bliss and thus reverberated that auspicious sound. Premānanda says, 'I can never have enough devotion to my beloved Gaurāṅga.' "

—Premānanda dāsa

gaurāṅgera duti pada yāra dhana-sampada
se jāne bhakati-rasa-sāra
gaurāṅgera madhura-līlā yāra karṇe praveśilā
hṛdaya nirmala bhela tāra
ye gaurāṅgera nāma laya tāra haya premodaya
tāre muin yai balihari
gaurāṅga-guṇete jhure nitya-līlā tāre sphure
se jana bhakati-adhikārī

gaurāṅgera saṅgi-gaṇe nitya-siddha kari māne
se yāya vrajendra-suta-pāśa
śrī-gauḍa-maṇḍala-bhūmi yebā jāne cintāmaṇi
tāra haya vraja bhūme vāsa

gaura-prema-rasārṇave se taraṅge yebā ḍube
se rādhā-mādhava-antaraṅga
gṛhe vā vanete thāke hā gaurāṅga' bole ḍāke
narottama māge tāra saṅga

"Whoever possesses the great treasure of the lotus feet of Gaurāṅga actually knows the essence of devotional ecstasy. As he hears the nectarean *līlā* of Lord Gaurāṅga, he becomes fully purified. He becomes absorbed in Gaurāṅga's Holy Name and divine love-ecstasy awakens in his heart. I congratulate him on such valuable success, saying, 'Bravo! you are credited with excellence.' As he cries remembering the qualities and glories of Śrī Gaurāṅga, the *nitya-līlā* of the Divine Couple is revealed in his heart, whereupon he is understood to be a qualified devotee who has attained pure devotional ecstasy.

"As he deeply understands and honors the intimate associates of Śrī Gaurāṅga as eternally liberated souls, he also gradually becomes liberated and ultimately attains the intimate association of the son of Nanda Mahārāja. As he feels at heart that the holy land of Śrī Gaura-maṇḍala is made of touchstone and enters into that consciousness, he resides on the transcendental plane of Vraja.

"As he dives deep into the infinite ocean of devotional ecstasy of Gaura, he becomes an intimate servitor of the Divine Couple Śrī Śrī Rādhā-Mādhava. Whether living as a householder or in a life of holy renunciation, Narottama dāsa always prays for the blessed association and grace of such pure devotees who are ever engaged in praying to Śrī Gaurāṅga, the personification of ecstatic love of Kṛṣṇa, calling out His Holy Name in the spontaneous rapture of devotional love."

—Narottama dāsa Ṭhākura, *Prārthanā*

kali-ghora timire garasala jaga jana
dharama karama rahu dūra
asādhane cintāmaṇi vidhi milāola āni
gorā baḍa dayāra ṭhākura

bhāire bhāi gorā-guṇa kahane nā yāya
kata śata ānana kata caturānana
baraṇiyā ora nāhi pāya

cāri-veda ṣaḍa-dara- śana kari adhyayana
se yadi gaurāṅga nāhi bhaje
bṛthā tāra adhyayana nayana bihīna jana
darapane andhe kibā kāje

veda vidyā dui kichui nā jānata
se yadi gaurāṅga jāne sāra
nayanānanda bhane sei se sakali jāne
sarva-siddhi karatale tāra

"When the dense nescience of the age of Kali covered the intelligence and consciousness of worldly people, their piety and spiritual principles receded far away. Despite this disqualification, Divine Providence brought to them the desire-fulfilling gem Cintāmaṇi Gaura, the Lord of all transcendental magnanimity and mercy. My dear brothers, the glories of Gaura are unlimited. Even great personalities of versatile intelligence like Lord Brahmā cannot find their end. If a person is well read and educated in the knowledge of the four Vedas and six philosophies but cannot appreciate Śrī Gaurāṅga, then all his education and accumulation of knowledge are simply useless, just as a mirror is of no use to a blind man. Nayanānanda says, 'A person who has no awareness of the Vedas or higher education but knows in his heart that Gaurāṅga is the divine essence of all truth must be considered truly wise, and all success will eventually come to him.'"

—Nayanānanda Prabhu

Śrīla Guru Mahārāja profoundly enjoyed the vast beauty of Gaura *premāsvādana* and *līlāsvādana*. Through this deep relish and contemplation in his middle age he composed another of his famous works known as *Prema-dhāma-deva-stotram*. What follows are some of the verses which were among his personal favorites:

kṛṣṇa kṛṣṇa kṛṣṇa kṛṣṇa kṛṣṇa nāma-kīrtanaṁ
rāma-rāma-gāna-ramya-divya-chanda-nartanam
yatra-tatra-kṛṣṇa-nāma-dāna-loka-nistaraṁ
prema-dhāma-devam eva naumi gaura-sundaram

"The Lord traveled to the holy places of pilgrimage in South India with the clever underlying compassionate intention of delivering the fallen souls. Appearing as a beautiful young renunciate, He distributed the sweet transcendental names of the Supreme Lord, singing *'Kṛṣṇa, Kṛṣṇa, Kṛṣṇa, Kṛṣṇa, Kṛṣṇa, Kṛṣṇa, Kṛṣṇa he'* as He strolled down the different pathways, entered temples, and visited homesteads. During His sacred pilgrimage, sometimes the Lord would be carried away by some indescribable, ineffable divine exaltation, and would sing *'Rāma, Rāma'* and dance gracefully with the most charming gestures and rhythms. Regardless of any time, place, circumstance, or personal qualification, He magnanimously delivered all those in South India who came in contact with Him by inspiring them to chant Kṛṣṇa's Holy Names with pure devotion. I sing with joy the unending glories of my golden Lord Gaurasundara, the beautiful divine abode of pure love." (22)

nyāsa-pañca-varṣa-pūrṇa-janma-bhūmi-darśanaṁ
koṭi-koṭi-loka-lubdha-mugdha-dṛṣṭi-karṣanam
koṭi-kaṇṭha-kṛṣṇa-nāma-ghoṣa-bheditāmvaraṁ
prema-dhāma-devam eva naumi gaura-sundaram

"When He returned to His birthplace Nadiyā after five long years of *sannyāsa,* millions of people rushed to see Him, feeling a most wonderful and irresistible love-attraction.

Deeply moved with eyes full of eagerness, they beheld their Lord who attracted their innermost heart of hearts. Excited by His ecstatic presence, there arose a continuous tumultuous uproar that spread in all directions and pierced the sky. To please their beloved Gaurāṅga, the people's voices repeatedly resounded the Holy Names of Kṛṣṇa. I sing with joy the unending glories of my golden Lord Gaurasundara, the beautiful divine abode of pure love." (34)

ārta-bhakta-śoka-śānti-tāpi-pāpi-pāvanaṁ
lakṣa-koṭi-loka-saṅga-kṛṣṇa-dhāma-dhāvanam
rāma-keli-sāgrajāta-rūpa-karṣaṇādaraṁ
prema-dhāma-devam eva naumi gaura-sundaram

"Śrī Gaurāṅgadeva soothed and pacified His devotees who were heartbroken due to the painful experience of His long separation, and forgave many offensive, anxiety-ridden persons such as Cāpāla Gopāla and others. Overwhelmed with wonderful attraction, He joyfully began to run towards Vṛndāvana, the abode of Kṛṣṇa. An ocean of people followed in His wake up to Rāmakeli where He was attracted by two of His eternal associates, Rūpa and his elder brother Sanātana, to whom He expressed His deep affection. I sing with joy the unending glories of my golden Lord Gaurasundara, the beautiful divine abode of pure love." (35)

vyāghra-vāraṇaina-vanya-jantu-kṛṣṇa-gāyakaṁ
prema-nṛtya-bhāva-matta-jhāḍakhaṇḍa-nāyakam
durga-vanya-mārga-bhaṭṭa-mātra-saṅga-saukaraṁ
prema-dhāma-devam eva naumi gaura-sundaram

"Leaving Rāmakeli, the Lord continued His journey towards Vṛndāvana. On the way He passed through Jārikhaṇḍa forest, where He inspired the jungle animals such as tigers, deer, elephants, and other forest creatures to sing with Him the Holy Names of Kṛṣṇa. Intoxicated by the wonderful nectarean experience of association with the Lord, the animals began to joyfully dance along with their newlyfound compassionate master toward whom they were drawn by an irresistible love. While He was madly absorbed in deep devotional ecstasy, the Lord easily and happily proceeded down the dense and impenetrable jungle path of Jārikhaṇḍa accompanied only by Balabhadra Bhaṭṭācārya. I sing with joy the unending glories of my golden Lord Gaurasundara, the beautiful divine abode of pure love." (36)

mādhavendra-vipralambha-māthureṣṭa-mānanaṁ
prema-dhāma-dṛṣṭakāma-pūrva-kuñja-kānanam
gokulādi-goṣṭha-gopa-gopīkā-priyaṅkaraṁ
prema-dhāma-devam eva naumi gaura-sundaram

"Lord Caitanya relished the mood of intensified love in separation (*vipralambha*) revealed from the core of the heart of Mādhavendra Puripāda in his composition *ayi dīna dayādranātha,* which describes Śrī Rādhikā's separation from Her beloved Kṛṣṇa after He had left for Mathurā. Intimately tasting its mood within His heart, Śrī Gaurāṅga revealed to His devotees that this mood of Śrīmatī Rādhikā is the zenith point of transcendental devotion. Before his very eyes he finally beheld Vṛndāvana, the abode of divine love of Kṛṣṇa, and became overwhelmed with the joy of His heart's satisfaction. The Lord was delighted to see the beautiful gardens and forest groves that had served as His playground for spiritual pastimes in a previous era. While visiting the twelve forests of Vṛndāvana such as Gokula Mahāvana, He displayed various affectionate dealings with the *gopīs* and *gopas* there. I sing with joy the unending glories of my golden Lord

Gaurasundara, the beautiful divine abode of pure love." (38)

prema-guñjanāli-puñja-puṣpa-puñja-rañjitaṁ
gīta-nṛtya-dakṣa-pakṣi-vṛkṣa-lakṣa-vanditam
go-vṛṣādi-nāda-dīpta-pūrva-moda-meduraṁ
prema-dhāma-devam eva naumi gaura-sundaram

"While strolling through the forest groves of Vṛndāvana, the beautiful flowers surrounded by bumble bees humming in sweet love-drones welcomed and entertained Him. The trees lining the forest groves harmoniously offered their respects to Him in unison with a variety of birds that were expertly dancing and singing in sheer delight. The Lord's mind became flooded by loving feelings remembering how the cows, calves, and oxen of the holy abode of Vṛndāvana would affectionately call for Him in a previous era. I sing with joy the unending glories of my golden Lord Gaurasundara, the beautiful divine abode of pure love." (39)

Śrīla Prabodhānanda Saraswatī was one of the all-time foremost devotees of Śrī Gaurāṅga. His exclusive and limitless devotion to Him has been revealed through his brilliant heart-touching compositions that have irresistibly attracted the hearts of all pure devotees of Śrī Caitanya Mahāprabhu. Śrīla Guru Mahārāja was no exception in this regard and would often relish these verses from Śrīla Prabodhānanda Saraswatī's *Caitanya-candrāmṛta* :

tāvad brahma-kathā vimukti-padavī tāvan na tiktī-bhavet
tāvac-cāpi viśṛṅkhalatvam ayate no loka-veda-sthitiḥ
tāvac-chāstra-vidāṁ mithaḥ kala-kalo nānā-bahir-vartmasu
śrī-caitanya-padāmbuja-priya-jano yāvan na dṛg-gocaraḥ

"The discussion of impersonal salvation attained by

means of the path of negation will not become bitter; the social and Vedic conventions will not be disrupted; and the intense controversy between the Vedic scholars regarding the importance of various external spiritual paths will continue only as long as a pure devotee who is beloved to Śrī Caitanyacandra and constantly engaged in relishing the nectar of His lotus feet does not appear before their eyes." (19)

yathā yathā gaura-padāravinde
vindeta bhaktiṁ kṛta-puṇya-rāśiḥ
tathā tathotsarpati hṛdy-akasmād
rādhā-padāmbhoja-sudhāmbu-rāsiḥ

"As a pious soul fortunately attains pure devotion to Gaura within his heart and becomes absorbed in rendering service to His lotus feet, to his delightful astonishment, the nectar-ocean of devotional ecstasy flowing from the lotus feet of Śrī Rādhikā suddenly floods his heart." (88)

strī-putrādi-kathāṁ jahur viṣayiṇaḥ śāstra-pravādaṁ budhā
yogīndrā vijahur marun niyamaka-kleśaṁ tapas tāpasāḥ
jñānābhyāsa-vidhiṁ jahuś ca yatayaś-caitanya-candre paraṁ
āviṣkurvati bhakti-yoga-padavīṁ naivānya āsīd rasaḥ

"Something most wonderful and miraculous has happened because the divine full moon Śrī Caitanyacandra has graciously illuminated the sky of everyone's heart, imbuing them with ambrosial transcendental love. Being deeply attracted by that, the materialists have given up talking about their wives, children, and mundane affairs. The *pandits* have given up arguing about scriptural conclusions, the *yogīs* have given up the difficulty of controlling their breath, the ascetics have given up their harsh austerities, and the impersonalist renunciates have given up their pursuit of impersonal philosophy. Now there is only one exclusive and superexcellent taste—the nectar of pure devotional service— compared to which, nothing else is attractive anymore." (113)

Although the following verses were not recorded, they were also among Śrīla Guru Mahārāja's favorites from *Caitanya-candrāmṛta.*

ānanda-līlāmaya-vigrahāya
hemābha-divya-cchavi-sundarāya
tasmai mahā-prema-rasa-pradāya
caitanya-candrāya namo namas te

"He who is the embodiment of divine bliss, whose form is decorated with the symptoms of ecstasy, who appears magnificently beautiful with a complexion as splendid as gold, and who benevolently gives in charity to all persons the ecstatic love for Kṛṣṇa, the highest divine perfection of life— I worship Him, my beloved Lord Caitanyacandra, again and again with full devotion." (11)

caitanyeti kṛpāmayeti paramodāreti nānā-vidha-
premāveśita-sarva-bhūta-hṛdayety-āścarya-dhāmann-iti
gaurāṅgeti guṇārṇaveti rasa-rūpeti sva-nāma-priyety
aśrāntaṁ mama jalpato janir iyaṁ yāyād iti prārthaye

"O Caitanya, O personification of divine knowledge, O supremely compassionate one, O Lord who fulfills the hearts of all living entities with the nectar of various devotional ecstasies, O wonderfully self-effulgent one, O golden-complexioned Lord, O ocean of transcendental qualities, O embodiment of divine love-ecstasy, O Lord who is fond of tasting Your own Holy Name—I pray that I may tirelessly continue chanting Your Holy Names throughout the rest of my life." (67)

kadā śaure gaure vapusi parama-prema-rasade
sad-eka-prāṇa-niṣkapaṭa-kṛta-bhāvo'smi bhavitā
kadā vā tasyālaukika-sad-anumānena mama hṛdy
akasmāt-śrī-rādhā-pada-nakha-maṇi-jyotir-udagāt

"O Kṛṣṇa, Your golden form is the life and soul of Your devotees. It is like a philanthropist who freely gives the nectar of divine love for You. When shall I wholeheartedly love this embodiment of nectar to my full satisfaction? I have finally understood the inner secret of this beautiful form: It is made of Śrī Rādhikā's mood and complexion. O, when will my heart be filled with the splendor of Her jewel-like toenails?" (68)

antar-dhvānta-cayaṁ samasta-jagatām unmūlayantī haṭhāt
premānanda-rasāmbudhiṁ niravadhi prodvelayantī balāt
viśvaṁ śītalayanty-atīva-vikalaṁ tāpa-trayeṇāniśaṁ
sāsmākaṁ hṛdaye cakāstu cakitaṁ caitanya-candra-cchaṭā

"The beautiful moonlight of Caitanyacandra powerfully dissipates the darkness from the heart of the world (*hṛdi jagat*). That moon continually creates tidal waves in the ocean of nectar which is the bliss of love of Kṛṣṇa, and brings coolness to the universe burning day and night with the threefold miseries of material existence. May that divine moonlight continually shine in our hearts." (75)

velāyāṁ lavaṇāmbudher madhurima-prāg-bhāva-sāra-sphural-
līlāyāṁ nava-ballavī-rasa-nidher-āveśayantī jagat
khelāyām api śaiśave nija-rucā viśvaika-sammohinī

mūrtiḥ kācana kañcana-dravamayī cittāyame rocate

"A form of molten gold enchants my heart. On the shore of the salt-water ocean that golden form manifests yet another ocean—that of the sweet mood of love-pastimes between the young *gopīs* and Kṛṣṇa, inundating the entire world of His devotees with that nectar. Ever since His childhood, this golden form has enchanted the whole spiritual world." (129)

And from the *Caitanya-caritāmṛta*:

kṛṣṇa-līlā amṛta-sāra tāra śata śata dhāra
daśa-dike vahe yāhā haite
se caitanya-līlā haya sarovara akṣaya
mano-haṁsa carāha tāhāte

"The pastimes of Kṛṣṇa are the quintessence of all divine nectar, and Caitanya-*līlā* is an inexhaustible lake of that nectar which, flowing in hundreds of streams, floods the hearts of the devotees in all directions. Therefore, O nectar-seeking friend, please let your mind swim in that lake like a regal swan."

—*C. C. Madhya* 25.271

Chapter Three

NĀMA-TATTVA

Like other *nāma-bhajanānandi* Vaiṣṇavas, Śrīla Guru Mahārāja also felt special devotional attraction and taste to relate to the Supreme Lord through His Holy Names. As he would contemplate or chant the Holy Names, he would feel a mystical closeness to the Divine Couple on the finer, subtler plane of his consciousness. From the example of Śrīmān Mahāprabhu and His followers as well as their emphatic instruction for all to take shelter of the Holy Name, Śrīla Guru Mahārāja felt special inspiration to engage in this sweet Nāma-*bhajan* and confidentially spoke of his realizations about the Holy Name. He explained that the sound and word form of Śrī Nāma directly connect one to the Supreme Lord. On the elevated stage of *śuddha-nāma-āsvādana,* the Holy Name becomes much more than sound or word. It combines with the other eternal aspects—*rūpa, guṇa, līlā, parikara,* and *vaiśiṣṭa*—to bring a pure devotee the unlimited joy of experiencing the total manifestation of the Lord. Meditating upon this auspicious potency of Śrī Kṛṣṇa *nāma-saṅkīrtana* and its special benediction to bless the people of *Kali-yuga* with the highest liberation, Śrīla Guru Mahārāja would recite the following verse:

kaler-doṣa-nidhe rājann-
asti hy eko mahān guṇaḥ
kīrtanād-eva kṛṣṇasya
mukta-saṅgaḥ paraṁ vrajet

"My dear king, despite the fact that *Kali-yuga* is an ocean of faults, there is still one unique quality about this age which is most beneficial for all. Simply by chanting, singing, or preaching the transcendental Holy Names and glories of the supreme *tattva* Kṛṣṇa, one can become free from material bondage and be promoted to His abode, the transcendental plane of perfection."

—*Śrīmad Bhāgavatam* 12.3.51

Śrīla Guru Mahārāja described how Śrīmān Mahāprabhu, with all adoration and enthusiasm, introduced this *yuga-dharma* of *nāma-saṅkīrtana* as the principal path for relating to Kṛṣṇa. Through his meditation on the following song, Śrīla Guru Mahārāja received a beautiful vision in his heart of the inauguration of Hari-*kīrtana* by Mahāprabhu at Śrīvāsaṅgan.

śrī-hari-vāsare hari-kīrtana vidhāna
nṛtya ārambhilā prabhu jagatera prāṇa
puṇya-vanta śrīvāsa-aṅgane śubhārambha
uṭhila kīrtana-dhvani gopāla govinda
mṛdaṅga mandirā bāje śaṅkha karatāla
saṅkīrtana saṅge sava haila miśāla
brahmāṇḍe uṭhila dhvani pūriyā ākāśa
caudikera amaṅgala yāya sava nāśa
caturdike śrī-hari-maṅgala-saṅkīrtana
madhye nāce jagannātha miśrera nandana
savāra aṅgete śobhe śrī-candana mālā
ānande nācaye save haiyā bibholā
nijānande nāce mahāprabhu viśvambhara
caraṇera tāli śuni ati manohara
bhāvāveśe mālā nāhi rahaye galāya
chiṇḍiyā paḍaye giyā bhakatera gāya
yāra nāmānande śiva basana nā jāne

yāra rase nāce śiva se nāce āpane
yāra nāme vālmikī haila tapodhana
yāra nāme ajāmila pāila mocana
yāra nāma śravaṇe saṁsāra bandha ghuce
hena prabhu avatari kali-yuge nāce
yāra nāma laye śuka nārada beḍāya
sahasra-badana prabhu yāra guṇa gāya
sarva-mahā-prāyaścitta ye prabhura nāma
se prabhu nācaye dekhe yata bhāgyavāna
śrī-kṛṣṇa-caitanya nityānanda cānda jāna
vṛndāvana dāsa tachu pada-yuge gāna

"Once, on the auspicious day of Ekādaśī in the house of Śrīvasa Pandit, Śrīmān Mahāprabhu inaugurated congregational *nāma-saṅkīrtana* with great enthusiasm, accompanied by His devotees and associates. Surging with divine ecstasy, Śrīmān Mahāprabhu, the life and soul of the universe, began to dance beautifully. The devotees surrounded Him, being deeply touched and inspired by such an ecstatic moment, and they also began to dance and sing the Holy Names like Gopāla and Govinda. The combined sound vibrations of *mṛdaṇga, mandirā* bells, *karatālas,* and *śaṅkha* in harmony with the congregational singing and dancing took everyone to the plane of transcendental delight. The holy vibration of *saṅkīrtana* filled the sky and spread through the ether all over the cosmic universal existence. Thus the atmosphere in all directions became purified and filled with auspiciousness by that divine sound.

"Everyone was decorated with fragrant sandalwood paste and beautiful garlands. The most wonderful rhythmic sound arose from the dancing footsteps of Śrīmān Mahāprabhu which captivated the minds of the devotees. As He continued dancing in His own self-born ecstasy, the swinging flower garlands around His neck began to fall, decorating the earth. The devotees beheld before their very eyes this rare and precious heart-captivating, ecstatic dance of the supreme *tattva*, Śrī Gaurāṅga, who is the most worshipable object of even the great personalities such as Lord Śiva, Śukadeva, Nārada, and others.

"Being totally overwhelmed and lost in the transcendental bliss of taking Mahāprabhu's Holy Name, Lord Śiva sometimes does not care for His formal appearance or for any obligation to retain His clothing, which sometimes falls down while He dances in the ecstasy of loving devotion. The pure devotees Śrī Śukadeva and Devarṣi Nārada are always blissfully engaged in relishing the nectar of Śrī Caitanyadeva's Holy Name and distributing it to suitable *jīva* souls wherever they travel. By chanting and meditating upon His Holy Name, Śrī Vālmikī became a great powerful *ṛṣi*, and Ajāmila attained pure liberation. Even Lord Anantadeva describes His unlimited glories with thousands of mouths. As one hears and takes Śrīmān Mahāprabhu's Holy Name with devotion, embracing its holy potency within the core of his heart, his existence becomes completely purified and he attains deliverance. The two brothers Śrī Kṛṣṇa Caitanya and Nityānanda Prabhu are my beloved masters, my life and soul. Thus Vṛndāvana dāsa sings this song of Their glorification and devotionally offers it at Their lotus feet."

—*Caitanya Bhāgavata, Madhya* 8

Śrīla Guru Mahārāja was also inspired by the *līlā* of Mahāprabhu taking the holy order of *sannyāsa*. Wishing to see His devotee admirers one last time before leaving Navadvīpa, Mahāprabhu aroused in their hearts a sudden sweet desire to see Him. Thus compelled, they gathered around their beloved Lord with loving devotion and He endearingly instructed them to always remain engaged in holy Kṛṣṇa-*saṅkīrtana.*

āpana galāra mālā sabākāre diyā
ājña karena gaura-hari kṛṣṇa kaha giyā
ki bhojane ki śayane kibā jāgaraṇe
aharniśa cinta kṛṣṇa balaha badane
yadi āmār prati sneha thāke sabākāra
kṛṣṇa binā keha kichu nā balibe āra
jagatera pitā kṛṣṇa ye nā bhaje bāpa
pitṛ-drohī pātakīra janme janme tāpa

"Blessing everyone with affection and placing His own flower garlands around their necks, Śrī Gaurahari instructed them to return to their homes and fully engage in the service and worship of Kṛṣṇa with all devotion. He said, 'Always engage in thinking, remembering, hearing, and speaking about Kṛṣṇa in all situations whether awake or sleeping, eating or resting. If you have affection for Me, please promise that you will never cultivate anything other than Kṛṣṇa. Kṛṣṇa is the benevolent father and supreme cause of the whole universe and all beings. One who deliberately avoids worshiping his own transcendental father is considered to be most fallen and suffers on account of this birth after birth.' "

—*Caitanya Bhāgavata, Madhya* 28.25-28

hare kṛṣṇa hare kṛṣṇa kṛṣṇa kṛṣṇa hare hare
hare rāma hare rāma rāma rāma hare hare
prabhu kahe kahilām ei mahāmaṇtra
ihā japa giyā save kariyā nirvvandha
ihā haite sarva-siddhi haibe savāra
sarvākṣaṇa bala ithe vidhi nāhi āra

"Śrīmān Mahāprabhu said, 'I Myself spoke this Hare Kṛṣṇa *mahā-maṇtra*, which is the most effective means of bringing divine benefit to the lives of the *jīva* souls. Go home and chant this holy *maṇtram* with all devotion. Everyone will attain all perfection by the grace of this magnanimous *maṇtra*. Therefore, chant and remember it all the time regardless of any rules and regulations.' "

—*Caitanya Bhāgavata, Madhya* 23.76-78

As Śrīla Guru Mahārāja's *bhajan* life unfolded, he experienced the variegated nature of the Holy Names. He explained that each and every Name of the Personality of Godhead has a special meaning and significance according to His aspects and pastimes. He especially relished the following verses:

nārāyaṇa parā-vedāḥ nārāyaṇa parākṣarā
nārāyaṇa parā-muktiḥ nārāyaṇa parāgatiḥ

O Nārāyaṇa—"O supreme personality of universal Truth, You are the origin and worshipable object of all divine knowledge.

O Nārāyaṇa—"O fundamental, causal cosmic potency who are by nature unlimited, all pervading, and omnipotent, You validate, maintain, and sustain the whole universe.

O Nārāyaṇa—"O bestower of pure liberation, You are attained by achieving an eternal devotional relationship with You.

O Nārāyaṇa—"You are the supreme ambrosial goal and shelter of life."

rāma-nārāyaṇānanta-mukunda-madhusūdanaḥ
kṛṣṇa-keśava-kaṁsāri-hare-vaikuṇṭha-vāmana

O Rāma—"O splendid ocean of divine pleasure and enchanter of the heart;

O Nārāyaṇa—O shelter of the universe and all life;

O Ananta—O unlimited omnipotent reality;

O Mukunda—O giver of pure liberation and perfection;

O Madhusūdana—O destroyer of that embodiment of all demoniac forces and elements, the demon Madhu;

O Kṛṣṇa, Keśava—O all-attractive personality of divine ambrosial beauty and ecstasy;

O Kaṁsāri—O destroyer of Kaṁsa, the embodiment of sinister powers;

O Hari—O You who steals away the devotees' hearts with Your unparalleled superexcellent attractiveness, unique loveliness, beauty, and glory;

O Vaikuṇṭha—O Supreme Reality who are transcendental to all limits and doubts, vulnerability and unsteadiness;

O Vāmana—O possessor of an unlimited range of abilities—

I worship You with all devotional love. May You compassionately embrace me in Your shelter."

harer-murāre madhu-kaiṭabhāre-gopāla-govinda-mukunda-śaure
yajñeśa-nārāyaṇa-kṛṣṇa-viṣṇu nirāśrayaṁ māṁ jagadīśa rakṣa

O Hari—"O You who captivates all hearts by Your unique divine loveliness, beauty, and glory;

O Murāri, Madhu-Kaiṭabhāri—O destroyer of the Mura, Madhu, and Kaiṭabha demons who represent demoniac consciousness of different patterns, inauspiciousness, and evil;

O Gopāla—O protector, nurturer, and maintainer of the universal creation;

O Govinda—O giver of delight to the heart and senses;

O Mukunda—O giver of blissful liberation;

O Śaure—O supreme almighty one;

O Yajñeśa—O exclusively worshipable object of all auspicious spiritual sacrifices and devotional endeavors;

O Nārāyaṇa—O eternal shelter of the universe and all life;

O Kṛṣṇa—O all-attractive reservoir of pleasure and ecstasy;

O Viṣṇu—O all-pervading supreme personality who are the preserver and maintainer of the whole creation;

O Jagadīśa—O supreme creator, controller, and enjoyer of the entire universe—

I have no shelter other than You. Please protect me, maintain me, and nurture me in the ambrosial embrace of Your shelter."

Śrīla Guru Mahārāja has always felt special liking for certain songs and verses describing the glories of the Holy Names such as: *Tuhun dayā sāgara, Śrī kṛṣṇa kīrtane yadi, Kṛṣṇa nāma dhare kata, Nikhila-śruti-mauli-ratna-mālā, Jayati jayati nāmānanda, Tava kathāmṛtaṁ tapta-jīvanaṁ, Nāma cintāmaṇiḥ kṛṣṇaś, Madhuraḥ-madhuram etan, Nāmaika yasya vāci, Śṛṇvatām-sva-kathāḥ kṛṣṇa,* and *Satāṁ prasaṅgān.*

Due to its special significance, the *Śikṣāṣṭakam* of Mahāprabhu was also very dear to him. He spoke extensively about it at different times, and the essence of his realizations are concisely presented here.

ceto-darpaṇa-mārjanaṁ bhava-mahā-dāvāgni-nirvāpaṇaṁ
śreyaḥ-kairava-candrikā-vitaraṇaṁ vidyā-vadhū-jīvanam
ānandāmbudhi-vardhanaṁ prati-padaṁ pūrṇāmṛtāsvādanaṁ
sarvātma-snapanaṁ paraṁ vijayate śrī-kṛṣṇa-saṅkīrtanam

"The Holy Name and glorification of Kṛṣṇa cleanse the mirror of the heart so that it becomes qualified and capable of receiving the true reflection of Kṛṣṇa's beauty. It extinguishes the fire of misery in the forest of birth and death. Just as an evening lotus blooms in the soothing rays of the moon, the heart with all good fortune begins to blossom in the nectar of the Holy Name. That blossomed heart then realizes that the glorification of Kṛṣṇa is actually the life-essence, ultimate meaning, and purpose of all transcendental knowledge and education. Finally revealing itself as the highest plane of divine love-servitude, *mādhurya-rasa-sevā,* that heart resplendently manifests as the life-nectar of a Vraja-*vadhū,* a damsel of Vraja. With this realization the soul awakens to its real inner treasure: a life of love with Kṛṣṇa. Tasting unlimited nectar again and again, the soul dives and surfaces in the ever-increasing ocean of ecstatic joy. All self-conceptions are fully satisfied and purified. Thus conquering one's heart and very existence with divine ambrosial pleasure, Kṛṣṇa-*saṅkīrtana* ever remains fully glorious and victorious."

—*Caitanya-caritāmṛta, Antya* 20.12

Śrīla Guru Mahārāja commented: "*Śrī Kṛṣṇa-saṅkīrtanam eva tatpadāśritānāṁ paramānukūlam*—Of all means favorable for cultivating the highest divine life in relation to Kṛṣṇa, the pure performance of Śrī Kṛṣṇa-*saṅkīrtana* is the best."

—*Śrī Prapanna-jīvanāmṛta* 3.2

Śrīla Guru Mahārāja also appreciated Ṭhākura Bhaktivinoda's illumination of this first verse of *Śikṣāṣṭakam* presented in his song *Pīta-varaṇa.* He fondly relished its esoteric meaning—that Kṛṣṇa-*saṅkīrtana* ultimately blesses a *jīva* soul with his *nitya-siddha-svarūpa,* the highest potential, of which is becoming a divine damsel whose nature and identity are eternally fulfilled with the ambrosial joy of engagement in the intimate service of the Divine Couple. With humility and devotion Śrīla Guru Mahārāja prayed to Nāma Prabhu and Mahāprabhu to attain that highest fortune.

nāmnām akāri bahudhā nija-sarva-śaktis
tatrārpitā niyamitaḥ smaraṇe na kālaḥ
etādṛśī tava kṛpā bhagavān mamāpi
durdaivam īdṛśam ihājani nānurāgaḥ

"O my Lord, Your Holy Name bestows auspiciousness upon all, and You have unlimited Names such as Kṛṣṇa and Govinda by which You reveal Yourself. In Your many Holy Names You have kindly invested all of Your transcendental potencies, and in chanting these Names there are no strict rules concerning time or place. Out of Your causeless mercy You have descended in the form of divine sound, but my great misfortune is that I have no love for Your Holy Name."

—*Caitanya-caritāmṛta, Antya* 20.16

Śrīla Guru Mahārāja commented: "*Śrī-kṛṣṇa-nāma-svarūpasya parama-pāvanatvaṁ, jīvasya durddaivañ-ca*—The Holy Name of Kṛṣṇa is always the supreme savior and purifier by nature, yet due to faithlessness, a *jīva*'s aversion to accepting that benediction remains the stumbling block on the way to his own highest fortune."

—*Śrī Prapanna-jīvanāmṛta* 8.3

In humility, considering himself as a most unfit devotee having no love for the Holy Name, Śrīla Guru Mahārāja would often feel very sad. The more he would feel sad, the more he would desperately embrace the shelter of the Holy Name and relate to it with increased devotional feelings. He described his realization that by continuously chanting and remembering of the Holy Name with a prayerful mood in the association of pure devotees, all misfortune gradually fades away.

Śrīla Guru Mahārāja explained that Śrīmān Mahāprabhu actually recited this verse feeling great love and devotion for the Holy Name of Kṛṣṇa while at the same time lamenting that He had no love for the Holy Name. Even though Śrīmān Mahāprabhu pointed out the misfortune of the conditioned *jīva*-soul through this verse, He also presented its deeper meaning that such feelings of misfortune in a pure devotee actually work in a very positive way. It brings on humility and lamentation which incite his desperation to relate to the Holy Name with more prayer and hankering. Such intense feelings arouse in his heart a deeper love and attraction for the Holy Name of Kṛṣṇa.

tṛṇād-api sunīcena
taror-iva sahiṣṇunā
amāninā mānadena
kīrtanīyaḥ sadā hariḥ

"One who knows himself as more insignificant than a blade of grass, who is as forbearing as a tree, and who gives due honor to others without desiring it for himself, is qualified to chant the glories of Lord Hari constantly."

—*Caitanya-caritāmṛta, Antya* 20.21

Śrīla Guru Mahārāja commented: "*Tatra sampatti-catuṣṭayaṁ paramānukūlam*— These four great qualities, like four precious jewels, are accepted and treasured as most favorable inner adornments for the performance of Hari-*kīrtana*."

—*Śrī Prapanna-jīvanāmṛta* 3.3

He described those qualities as follows:

"*Humility*—Conjoined with *śraddhā* (unalloyed faith) and devotion, these represent the most valuable capital of a pure spiritual seeker. One great enemy of *śraddhā* is false ego. As long as the mind and heart possess false ego, they cannot feel any taste or experience the transcendental nature of the Holy Name. It is most important that *Hari-kīrtana* be performed with a mind free from false ego. Sincere humility, born from one's knowledge of the *jīva*'s infinitesimal position, is a great friend who protects and nurtures one's spiritual life. Therefore humility represents the noble principle of an egoless approach to the Supreme Lord.

"*Tolerance*—Being as tolerant as a tree represents the spiritual qualities of forgiveness, nonviolence, peacefulness, affectionate nurturing, giving no trouble to anyone, and selfless happiness in helping others. This powerful quality of tolerance or forbearance becomes a natural part of the life of an advanced devotee. Cultivating this holy power in himself, he remains unaffected by the disturbances created in general society and thereby stays firmly situated in the ideal performance of *Hari-kīrtana*.

"*Not accepting honor*—The desire for receiving personal honor from others without the real interest of Kṛṣṇa simply engenders selfish greed, false pride, and the superiority complex of underestimating others. As long as one's heart is possessed by such greed and eagerness for honor, he cannot feel peace and therefore cannot steadily devote himself to Kṛṣṇa and His Holy Name.

"*Giving respect*—The devotee offers all respect to others, knowing that Kṛṣṇa is present in them as Supersoul. But he does not become dependent or personally entangled with them upon receiving any futile honor in return. Having no separate, selfish motive he becomes qualified to serve Kṛṣṇa and engage others accordingly."

In this way Śrīla Guru Mahārāja explained that humility, tolerance, reluctance for receiving personal honor, and offering due honor to others are the four great qualities which make one internally powerful and promote the unconditional spirit of dedication necessary to purely engage in *Hari-kīrtana.*

nayanaṁ galad-aśru-dhārayā
vadanaṁ gadgada-ruddhayā girā
pulakair nicitaṁ vapuḥ kadā,
tava nāma-grahaṇe bhaviṣyati

"My dear Lord, when will My eyes be decorated with tears that constantly glide down as I chant Your Holy Name? When will My voice falter and My body be thrilled in transcendental ecstasy as I chant Your Holy Name?"

—*Caitanya-caritāmṛta, Antya* 20.36

Śrīla Guru Mahārāja commented: "*Vipralambhe milana-siddhau nāma-bhajanānukūlyam*—Pure adoration of the Holy Name in the love-mellows of the pain of separation is favorable for achieving blissful union with the Supreme Lord."

—*Śrī Prapanna-jīvanāmṛta* 3.26

He explained that as Kṛṣṇa's Holy Names are nondifferent from Him, They are actually the source of all transcendental nectar; but it may not always be easy in the stage of *sādhanā* to receive that nectar because of offenses or inadequate faith. Still, one should never give up his genuine aspiration for that nectarean experience because continuous prayer to the Lord ultimately draws His compassion, and thus one soon becomes blessed by tasting the ecstasy of transcendental love while chanting the Holy Name. Śrīla Guru Mahārāja further explained that this verse has a different relevance when applied to a *mahābhāgavata*. Such a prayerful mood in a pure devotee who is actually tasting the ecstasy of hankering in separation from the divine Holy Name must be understood in a distinct way: his prayer is full of acute feelings as he relates to the Holy Name with the saddened love-mellows of *vipralambha*-union in separation. Chanting in this exalted mood ultimately leads him to the ever-cherished, ever-longed-for ecstasy of *sambhoga*, union in union. In this state, the wonderful symptoms of divine love-ecstasy described in this verse automatically manifest throughout his heart and existence. In this mood of *vipralambha*, Śrīla Guru Mahārāja also implored the Lord: "O Kṛṣṇa, when will Your causeless mercy enable me to attain the ambrosial experience of love for You through the chanting of Your Holy Name? When will that day be mine?"

Such *śuddha-nāma-āsvādana* (relishing the mellows of the pure Name) flowed continuously through Śrīla Guru Mahārāja's *bhajan* life. He would especially relish this verse:

tuṇḍe tāṇḍavinī ratiṁ vitanute tuṇḍāvalī-labdhaye
karṇa-kroḍa-kaḍambinī-ghaṭayate-karṇārbudebhyaḥ spṛhām
cetaḥ-prāṅgaṇa-saṅginī vijayate sarvendriyāṇāṁ kṛtiṁ
no jāne janitā kiyadbhir-amṛtaiḥ kṛṣṇeti varṇa-dvayī

"I do not know how much nectar the two syllables '*kṛṣṇa*' have blessed me with. When I chant the Holy Name of Kṛṣṇa, I feel the exquisite nectarean taste of its ecstatic dance within my mouth, and that taste makes me desire many, many mouths. When that Name enters my ears, I desire many millions of ears out of intense eagerness to relish its sweetness; and finally, entering the courtyard of my heart, it reveals Kṛṣṇa's full-bloomed form, beauty, qualities, glories, and pastimes—captivating and conquering all of my mind, heart, and senses by its unlimited, ambrosial pleasure."

—*Vidagdha Mādhava* 1.12

Absorbed in devotional dedication, honoring the exalted *bhāva* of Śrī Rādhā Ṭhākurānī, Śrīla Guru Mahārāja felt that this verse was spoken by Her as She described *Her* unlimited nectarean experience with the two syllables of Kṛṣṇa's Name.

Throughout history, different pure Vaiṣṇavas have realized some of the variegated esoteric meanings of the *mahā-mantra*. They discovered their own particular taste in variegated love-mellows while chanting and meditating upon that *mantra* with pure devotion. Śrīla Guru Mahārāja also had some spontaneous revelations at certain blissful moments of his life. Out of humility he kept them confidential and spoke of them only to a very few of his intimate devotees.

Hare Kṛṣṇa Hare Kṛṣṇa Kṛṣṇa Kṛṣṇa Hare Hare
Hare Rāma Hare Rāma Rāma Rāma Hare Hare

The following revealed meaning is composed of the spontaneous responses between the Divine Couple (Mahābhāva and Rasarāja) during an intimate pastime as They address each other.

Hare—"O My beloved Rādhe...."

Kṛṣṇa—"O My beloved Kṛṣṇa...."

Hare—"O My beloved queen, You instantly steal away My heart by Your superexcellent exquisite beauty and devotional qualities."

Kṛṣṇa—"O all-attractive one, You irresistibly attract My heart and soul by Your ever-excelling beauty and ambrosial nature."

Kṛṣṇa, Kṛṣṇa—"O dearmost object of My devotion, O personified love-ecstasy Kṛṣṇa, please continue attracting Me towards You more and more intimately."

Hare, Hare—"O dearest goddess, object of My adoration Rādhe, please take more and more of My heart by Your intimate love."

Hare—"O Rādhe, My dearest beloved...."

Rāma—"O reservoir and giver of nectarean pleasure, Kṛṣṇa...."

Hare—"O beautiful goddess Rādhe, You utterly capture and captivate My heart...."

Rāma—"O Kṛṣṇa, Lord of My life, please take My body, mind, and heart, and enjoy Me to Your utmost satisfaction...."

Rāma, Rāma—"O Rāma, giver of pleasure and ecstasy, My dearest beloved Kṛṣṇa, please flood My heart with nectarean pleasure by enjoying Me eternally."

Hare Hare—"O Rādhe, take Me more deeply into the core of Your devoted heart and make Me eternally relish Your transcendental love, the all-fulfilling ambrosia of My life."

Chapter Four

KṚṢṆA-TATTVA

Śrīla Guru Mahārāja had a unique way of discovering the highest significance of the descriptions about Kṛṣṇa and entering into their deep esoteric meanings. He loved to define Kṛṣṇa in his own favorite English term 'Reality the Beautiful.'

Other terms he was particularly fond of are as follows:

1. *Svayaṁ Bhagavān*—The Supreme Personality of Divine Truth; the all-pervading universal Reality; the omnipotent, omniscient, and omnipresent enjoyer of all opulence

2. *Bhajanīya-guṇa-viśiṣṭa*—One who cannot but be worshiped due to His unlimited qualities of power, charm, and beauty

3. *Sat-Cid-Ānanda Vigraha*—The Supreme Personality of Godhead who is the embodiment of all Eternity, Truth, Goodness, Knowledge, Awareness, *Śakti*, and Bliss

4. *Satyam Śivam Sundaram*—The highest truth, auspiciousness, pure liberation, and beauty

5. *Advaya-jñāna tattva*—The Supreme Truth who is the goal of all perfect knowledge of nondualism

6. *Akhila-rasāmṛta-mūrti* (*Raso vai saḥ*)—The personification of all ambrosial ecstasy

7. *Ānanda-līlā Puruṣottama*—The divine male form eternally decorated with blissful playfulness and pleasure-pastimes

8. *Rasopyasya param dṛṣṭvā nivartate*—He who, when seen as the supreme *rasa-tattva*, withdraws His devotees' hearts from all other attractions

9. *Aprākṛta Madana*—The god of transcendental amorous love.

Śrīla Guru Mahārāja found that the stream of devotion to Śrīmān Mahāprabhu took his heart to the world of Kṛṣṇa-*prema*, which inundated his life with an unprecedented taste of ecstasy. He experienced the multifarious ways of nectarean love for Kṛṣṇa as tasted by his *guru-varga*, which inspired in him an intense hankering for further admittance into devotional service to Kṛṣṇa. He experienced great happiness in worshiping Śrī Kṛṣṇa through some of these selected songs and verses: *Gopīnātha mama nivedana śuna, Janama saphala tār, Suna he rasika jana, Yamunā puline,* the songs of *Kārpaṇya-pañjikā, Ambudāñjanendra-nīla, Namāmīśvaraṁ,* and others.

Śrīla Guru Mahārāja took sublime satisfaction and pleasure in glorifying Śrī Nanda Mahārāja, who captured, by his *śuddha vātsalya-prema,* the Paraṁ Brahma, Kṛṣṇa, as his own beloved son.

śrutim apare smṛtim itare
bhāratam anye bhajantu bhava-bhītāḥ
aham iha nandaṁ vande
yasyālinde paraṁ brahma

"Those who fear material existence worship the Vedas; some worship the *Smṛti*; and others worship the *Mahābhārata*. But I am drawn to the worship of Mahārāja Nanda, because I see that the Supreme Cosmic Truth Paraṁ Brahma is playing in his courtyard as a baby boy."

—Śrī Raghupati Upādhyāya, *Śrī Caitanya-caritāmrta Madhya* 19.96
—Śrīla Rūpa Goswāmī's *Padyāvalī* 126

Śrīla Guru Mahārāja commented: "*Vraja-rasa śreṣṭhatvam*—The quality and taste of the devotional pleasure of Vraja is always superexcellent."

—*Prapanna-jīvanāmṛta* 3.20

The following two verses were spontaneously composed by Śrīmān Mahāprabhu as He relished the mood of *sakhya* and *vātsalya rasa*. Śrīla Guru Mahārāja explained that the sweet purpose of Kṛṣṇa's playful stealing missions was actually to steal away the minds and hearts of His devotees with His incomparable charm and beauty. Imbued with the mood of Śrīmān Mahāprabhu, Guru Mahārāja also eagerly prayed to be embraced in the sweet shelter of Bāla Kṛṣṇa, His mother, and the other *gopīs* who eternally relish Kṛṣṇa's beautiful pastimes, those *līlās* which ever nourish their lives with divine nectar.

dadhi-mathana-ninādais-tyakta-nidraḥ prabhāte
nibhṛta-padam agāraṁ ballavīnāṁ praviṣṭaḥ
mukha kamala-samīrair-āśu nirvāpya dīpān
kavalita-navanītaḥ pātu māṁ bāla-kṛṣṇaḥ

"Upon awakening early in the morning and hearing the sound of churning milk, the beautiful child Kṛṣṇa got up and stealthily entered the homes of the *gopīs* who were engaged in preparing butter. He swiftly blew out the lamps and with great dexterity grabbed a handful of their freshly-made butter! By such sweet, charming, playful pastimes, Bāla Kṛṣṇa nurtured and sustained the lives of His devotees with divine pleasure. May He also fondly maintain Me in the same way."

—*Śrī Caitanyacandra*

Śrīla Guru Mahārāja commented: "*Vraja-līlasya śrī-kṛṣṇasya pālakatvam prabhāva-mayam*—Śrī Kṛṣṇa, the Lord of the divine pastimes of Vraja, is the most powerful maintainer and protector. By the sweet loving nature of such pastimes, He nurtures devotion to Him more and more."

—*Prapanna-jīvanāmṛta* 6.12

savye pānau niyamita-ravaṁ kiṅkinī-dāma dhṛtvā
kubjī-bhūya prapada-gatibhir-manda-mandaṁ vihasya
akṣṇor-bhaṅgyā vihasita-mukhīr-vārayan sammukhīnā
mātuḥ paścād-aharata harir-jātu haiyaṁ gavīnam

"Stifling the sound of His golden waistbells with His left hand, child Hari stealthily crept into the milk-churning area with a cute smile, gesturing silence with His eyes to the *gopīs* who were finding it difficult to check their laughter, and stole freshly-made butter right from behind His mother's back!"

—*Śrī Caitanyacandra*

The *nāma, rūpa, guṇa, līlā, parikara,* and *vaiśiṣṭa* of Kṛṣṇa, Reality the Beautiful, were all very dear to Śrīla Guru Mahārāja's heart. The verse that follows is a specific verse from *Śrīmad Bhāgavatam* which describes His charming visual beauty. Śrīla Guru Mahārāja, by his inner subjective realization, fully accepted and embraced this form of Kṛṣṇa as the eternally endearing, transcendental humanlike form of the Supreme Universal Reality. Appearing in a transcendental dimension of this earthly plane in such a beautiful form, Śrī Kṛṣṇa irresistibly attracted the hearts of all fortunate beings, fulfilling them with ecstatic love for Himself. Contemplating this form of Kṛṣṇa decorated with cosmic and natural beauty, Śrīla Guru Mahārāja used to stay immersed in blissful moods for hours.

śyāmaṁ hiraṇya-paridhiṁ vanamālya-barha-
dhātu-pravāla-naṭa-veṣam anuvratāṁse
vinyasta-hastam itareṇa dhunānam abjaṁ
karṇotpalālaka-kapola-mukhābja-hāsam

"His complexion was the color of a blue raincloud, and His garment was golden. Sporting a peacock feather on His head, colored minerals decorating His body, wearing sprigs of flower buds and a garland of forest flowers, He was artistically dressed like a beautiful dancing actor. He rested one hand upon the shoulder of a friend, and with the other He twirled a lotus. Delicate lilies adorned His ears, and His curling hair gently caressed the cheeks of His lotus face which was sweetly smiling."

—*Śrīmad Bhāgavatam* 10.23.22

Śrīla Guru Mahārāja explained that all kinds of divine love attraction ultimately culminate in *mādhurya rati*. He identified with the esoteric flow of this *mādhurya bhāva* that manifested through his Gaura-Rūpa-Vinoda-Saraswatī-*dhārā* and relished the form of Kṛṣṇa as described through the following verses:

barhāpīḍaṁ naṭa-vara-vapuḥ karṇayoḥ karṇikāraṁ
bibhrad vāsaḥ kanaka-kapiśaṁ vaijayantīṁ ca mālām
randhrān veṇor-adhara-sudhayā-pūrayan gopa-vṛndair
vṛndāraṇyaṁ sva-pada-ramaṇaṁ prāviśad-gīta-kīrtiḥ

"His head decorated with a peacock feather ornament, small *karnikara* flowers on His ears, wearing a shimmering golden-yellow garment and a *vaijayanti-mālā* around His neck, Lord Kṛṣṇa exhibited His exquisitely beautiful form as the most attractive dancer as He entered the forest of Vṛndāvana. Filling the holes of His flute with the nectar of His lips, He enchanted the land of the forests with great pleasure at every step, and everyone sang His glories."

—*Śrīmad Bhāgavatam* 10.21.5

veṇuṁ kvaṇantam aravinda-dalāyatākṣam-
barhāvataṁsam asitāmbuda-sundarāṅgam
kandarpa-koṭi-kamanīya-viśeṣa-śobhaṁ
govindam ādi-puruṣaṁ tam ahaṁ bhajāmi

"I worship Govinda, the primeval Lord, who is adept in playing on His flute, with blooming eyes like lotus petals and His head bedecked with a peacock's feather, with a figure of beauty tinged with the hue of blue clouds, and His unique loveliness charming millions of Cupids."

—*Brahma Saṁhitā* 30

ālola-candraka-lasad-vanamālya-vaṁśī-
ratnāṅgadaṁ praṇaya-keli-kalā-vilāsam
śyāmaṁ tri-bhaṅga-lalitaṁ niyata-prakāśaṁ
govindam ādi-puruṣaṁ tam ahaṁ bhajāmi

"I worship Govinda, the primeval Lord, around whose neck is swinging a garland of flowers beautified with the moon-locket, whose two hands are adorned with the flute and jeweled ornaments, who always revels in pastimes of love, and whose graceful threefold-bending form of Śyāmasundara is eternally manifest."

—*Brahma Saṁhitā* 31

This next verse is an earnest appeal to Kṛṣṇa for help in an extremely helpless condition. It is spoken by Queen

Draupadī while she was being insulted in the open assembly of the Kauravas. She beseeched her benevolent friend in all desperation and thus great help came from Him in that moment of dire necessity.

he kṛṣṇa dvārakā-nātha he gopījana-vallabha
dāsyāste kṛpaṇāyāyā sakhe darśaya sannidhiṁ

"O all-attractive Lord Kṛṣṇa, O king of Dvārakā, O beloved Lord of the *gopīs*, please kindly appear before me, your maidservant. O beloved friend, I am in great need of Your mercy at this time."

—*Mahābhārata*

Śrīla Guru Mahārāja pointed out that Queen Draupadi first addressed Kṛṣṇa as Dvārakānātha, the king and protector of the residents of Dvārakā, but then addressed Him as Gopījana-vallabha, the ever-cherished eternal beloved of the *gopīs*. According to Śrīla Guru Mahārāja, as she called out 'Gopījana-vallabha,' she actually surrendered herself to Lord Kṛṣṇa in the unconditional and exclusive way of the Vraja *gopīs*, whereupon Kṛṣṇa immediately saved her from that most humiliating situation. Through this verse, Śrīla Guru Mahārāja relished the *rasika* beauty of the unconditional, exclusive, loving surrender of Queen Draupadi to Lord Kṛṣṇa. His heart was so attracted to this divine beauty that he himself often prayed to his beloved Kṛṣṇa in the essence of this mood.

Through this next verse, Śrīla Guru Mahārāja relished the esoteric and intimate loving activities between Paraṁ Brahma Kṛṣṇa and the *gopīs*, the damsels of Vraja-*dhama* who conquered His heart by their exclusive loving dedication.

Śrīla Guru Mahārāja cautioned that this kind of *līlā* is transcendental to worldly love even though it may sometimes appear similar (*prākṛta vat na tu prākṛtam*).

kaṁ prati kathayitum īśe
samprati ko vā pratītim āyātu
go-pati-tanayā-kuñje
gopa-vadhūṭī-viṭaṁ brahma

"To whom can I speak? Who will believe me when I say that Kṛṣṇa, the Supreme Personality of Godhead, hunted the *gopīs* in the bushes on the banks of the Yamuna? In this way the Absolute Truth beautifully revealed His pastimes."

—Śrī Raghupati Upādhyāya, *C. C. Madhya* 19.98

—*Padyāvalī* 99

Śrīla Guru Mahārāja deeply relished the internal meaning of this verse, which is: "O Paraṁ Brahma Kṛṣṇa, You are the Supreme Absolute Truth and omniscient Reality. You are self-fulfilled and transcendental to the limited conception. You are by nature infinitely mystical, and therefore You are described as unknown and unknowable by the limited human perception. You simply remain beyond anyone's reach. It is only Your incredible love-seeking nature that attracts You to perform intimate *līlā* with Your devotees. Simultaneously, the love of Your exalted devotees captivates and conquers You. It is indeed this loving dedication of the Vraja *gopīs* and Your love-seeking nature which made You hunt after them in the bushes on the bank of the Yamunā. My dear friend, who can comprehend Your transcendental *līlā* from the standpoint of worldly morality? To be sought by You in such an intimate loving relationship is the inconceivably highest fortune of life."

The following verse from the *Bhramara Gītā* (Song to the Bumblebee) was spoken by Śrīmatī Rādhikā in spontaneous remembrance and glorification of Her beloved Kṛṣṇa while She was experiencing *vipralambha-daśā*.

yad-anucarita-līlā-karṇa-pīyūṣa-vipruṭ-
sakṛd-adana-vidhūta-dvandva-dharmā vinaṣṭāḥ
sapadi gṛha-kuṭumvaṁ dīnam utsṛjya dīnā
bahava iha vihaṅgā bhikṣu-caryāṁ caranti

"The transcendental *līlā* of Śrī Kṛṣṇa is great nectar for the ears. Those who relish just a single drop of that nectar even once have their dualistic material attachments utterly ruined. Many such persons have suddenly given up their nondevotional homes and families as futile and have come to Vṛndāvana, like birds freed from their cages. Becoming detached from their material life, those devotees have taken up the path of renunciation and are accepting alms just to maintain their lives on this plane. In this way they continue to search for Him, the all-perfect fulfillment of life."

—*Śrīmad Bhāgavatam* 10.47.18

The internal meaning of *bhikṣu caryāṁ caranti* according to Śrīla Guru Mahārāja is that those persons mentioned in this verse did not just beg some alms to make a living, but actually begged with all their hearts for a glimpse of mercy from their beloved master Kṛṣṇa, who was their only shelter. The deep purport of this verse was very significant in the personal life of Śrīla Guru Mahārāja. He remembered the turning point in his own life when he began to know more about the *anucarita-līlā* of Kṛṣṇa, becoming absorbed and overwhelmed in its nectarean taste. Thus He accepted the holy renounced order to remain exclusively dedicated to the deeper search and cultivation of that divine life. His hankering never ceased; rather, it intensified to an even greater degree in his last days. Humbly following in the line of Śrī Rādhikā's feelings, Her exclusive servitor Śrīla Guru Mahārāja recited the aforesaid verse as a great beggar of transcendental grace and *rasa*.

Even though there is no particular mention in *Śrīmad Bhāgavatam* about the name of the Vraja *gopī* who spoke this following verse, according to Śrīla Guru Mahārāja's realization, it was none other than Śrīmatī Rādhikā, crying out in the intense pain of separation from Her beloved Kṛṣṇa.

he nātha he ramā-nātha
vraja-nāthārti-nāśana
magnam uddhara govinda
gokulaṁ vṛjinārṇavāt

"O My beloved master, owner, protector, and maintainer! O beloved master of the goddess of fortune! O master of Vraja! O destroyer of all suffering! Govinda, kindly lift Your Gokula out of the ocean of distress in which it is drowning."

—*Śrīmad Bhāgavatam* 10.47.52

Śrīla Guru Mahārāja described that after Śrī Kṛṣṇa left Vṛndāvana for Mathurā, the Vraja *gopīs*, especially Śrī Rādhikā, were all immersed in the ocean of intense separation. Śrī Kṛṣṇa, being their eternal life and soul, fully knew their inexplicable devotional pain of heart and at one point He also became afflicted by the same painful feelings. As He remembered His intimate pastimes with them and their exclusive loving devotion to Him, He became overwhelmed with great pangs of separation. He then decided to send His dearmost servitor Uddhava to them with a message expressing His heart's anguish. Upon knowing that Uddhava was the messenger of Kṛṣṇa, the *gopīs,* headed by Śrī Rādhikā, surrounded him with great inquisitiveness, asking him all about Kṛṣṇa. They were so overwhelmed knowing that Kṛṣṇa had sent a message to them that the burning fire of their heart's separation from their dearmost beloved fully erupted. Due to the upsurging conflagration in Her most tender heart, this verse was then spoken by Śrī Rādhikā. She did not even address Uddhava but called out to Kṛṣṇa directly in unbearable agony, and implored Him to relieve all those who were helplessly drowning in the ocean of distress in separation from Him.

The following is a similar kind of verse quoted by Śrīla Guru Mahārāja in *Prapanna-jīvanāmṛta* describing the same intense *vipralambha prema* of Śrī Rādhikā imbued with all humility caused by feelings of emptiness due to separation.

hā nātha ramaṇa preṣṭha, kvāsi kvāsi mahā-bhuja
dāsyās te kṛpaṇāyā me, sakhe darśaya sannidhim

"O beloved Lord, O loving consort, O giver of pleasure, O dearmost hero, where are You? I am Your poor maidservant who is feeling completely lost and empty without You. Please bring Me close to You."

Śrīla Guru Mahārāja commented: "*Vrajendranandana-virahe taj-jīviteśvaryāḥ svayaṁ-rūpāyā api dāsīvat kārpaṇyam*—Even Śrī Rādhikā, who is the heroine and beloved goddess of Vrajendra-Nandana Kṛṣṇa, humbly petitions the Lord in separation from Him like a maidservant."

—*Prapanna-jivanāmṛta* 8.25

Śrīla Guru Mahārāja specifically pointed out the exalted humility of Śrī Rādhikā. In separation on the plane of transcendence, such humility appears due to intense hankering for the beloved's association, and this hankering is often characterized by such sweet imploring appeals. Śrīla Guru Mahārāja, being an eternal follower-servitor of Śrī Rādhikā under the guardianship of Śrī Rūpa-Saraswatī, became fully absorbed in this mood and prayed to Kṛṣṇa with an all-humble appeal to also relieve him from the feelings of great emptiness due to separation and to take him back to the divine abode of *nitya-līlā*.

Śrīla Guru Mahārāja's devotional humility, imbued with the sweet sadness of separation from Gaura Kṛṣṇa, is most marked by his murmuring of the following verses from Śrīmān Mahāprabhu's *Śikṣāṣṭakam*. They reveal Mahāprabhu's mood of *śaranāgati*—pure devotion and intense hankering to eternally remain embraced within the bliss of Kṛṣṇa-*prema* in intimate servitude. One of the six limbs of *śaranāgati* is rejecting that which is unfavorable to pure devotion. Without following this principle, unalloyed devotion to Kṛṣṇa cannot be attained.

Śrīla Guru Mahārāja entered into this mood to approach his beloved Lord Kṛṣṇa, and while tasting this he also adored Mahāprabhu as the nondifferent combination of the Divine Couple.

na dhanaṁ na janaṁ na sundarīṁ, kavitāṁ vā jagadīśa kāmaye
mama janmani janmanīśvare, bhavatād bhaktir-ahaitukī tvayi

"O Lord, I do not ever desire wealth, followers, popularity, a beautiful spouse, or the fame of scholarship for my personal enjoyment. Any such worldly promotion and sense gratification only harm my true interest, which is my ever-cherished relationship with You. These things can tempt me away from You, my highest fortune, and keep me addicted to selfish enjoyment. Even salvation is empty without You, for You are my beloved master and only solace; I therefore pray for unmotivated devotion and service to You birth after birth."

—*Caitanya-caritāmṛta, Antya* 20.29

Śrīla Guru Mahārāja commented on the text "*Na dhanam*": "*Prātikūlya-varjjana-saṅkalpādarśaḥ*—This is the ideal determination for rejecting that which is unfavorable to pure devotion."

—*Prapanna-jivanāmṛta* 4.2

ayi nanda-tanuja kiṅkaram patitaṁ māṁ viṣame bhavāmbudhau
kṛpayā tava-pāda-paṅkaja-sthita-dhūlī-sadṛṣaṁ vicintaya

"O son of Mahārāja Nanda, by my constitutional nature as Your marginal potency, I am Your eternal loving servitor. You generously gave me free will, but by misusing that valuable freedom, I gradually became tempted by selfish enjoyment under the influence of *mahā-māyā*. Instead of serving You, I have fallen into the ocean of birth and death. Kindly save me from this ocean of misery and consider me as a particle of dust at Your lotus feet."

—*Caitanya-caritāmṛta, Antya* 20.32

Śrīla Guru Mahārāja explained that on the plane of perfection (*cintāmaṇi dhāma*), every particle of dust is actually a highly qualified spiritual being, and the lotus feet of Kṛṣṇa are the supreme ambrosial solace of their individual lives. He therefore prayed to be accepted as the Lord's tiny servitor.

Such a position is considered so highly relishable that Śrīla Guru Mahārāja commented: "*Śrī-bhagavato bhakta-bhāvenāśraya-prārthanam*—Even the Supreme Lord (Caitanya)

Himself prays for shelter in the mood of a devotee."

—*Prapanna-jīvanāmṛta* 6.3

He also felt that Śrīmān Mahāprabhu's addressing Kṛṣṇa as Nanda-tanuja endearingly characterized the bond of love and compassion which the Lord has for His pure devotee. It is this special characteristic that made Him appear as the son of Nanda Mahārāja. By uttering the name 'Nanda-tanuja,' Mahāprabhu also revealed that it was specifically to Vraja-*tattva* Kṛṣṇa that He was praying.

Understanding all the intrinsic characteristics of this mood, Śrīla Guru Mahārāja recognized the meaning of this verse as the conception of *goptṛtve varaṇam*—acceptance of the Lord as one's supreme protector. Feeling lonely in separation, he personally prayed in the mood of Mahāprabhu: "O Nanda-tanuja, You are very affectionate to Your devotees, and I cannot but draw Your kind attention. I am miserable in this mortal world without You. Please protect and maintain this unqualified humble servitor beneath the shelter of Your lotus feet."

Śrīla Guru Mahārāja felt that the last two verses of *Śikṣāṣṭakam* represent the mood and character of Śrī Rādhikā's exalted divine love in *vipralambha* for Śrī Kṛṣṇa. Imbued with Her *bhāva*, Mahāprabhu sang them while tasting their inner sweetness. Śrī Rādhikā, describing Her divine loneliness and desperation, petitions Kṛṣṇa:

yugāyitaṁ nimeṣeṇa, cakṣuṣā prāvṛṣāyitam
śūnyāyitaṁ jagat sarvaṁ govinda-viraheṇa me

"O Govinda, tears stream from My eyes—like rain—because without You the whole world is empty, and a moment seems like a great millennium."

—*Caitanya-caritāmṛta, Antya* 20.39

Śrīla Guru Mahārāja commented: "*Govinda-virahe sarva-śūnyatayā aty-anāthavad-dīrgha-duḥkha-bodha-rūpa-prema-ceṣṭā* —To the pure devotees in this stage, everything appears vacant in separation from Govinda. They feel shelterless, and their pure love and extreme longing for Govinda's association manifests in the form of prolonged sadness."

—*Prapanna-jīvanāmṛtam* 8.28

Holding this mood of devotional hankering with high respect, Śrīla Guru Mahārāja tasted its esoteric sweetness in all humility. He often quoted a verse from *Śrī Caitanya-caritāmṛta* explaining the inconceivably wonderful nature of this *vipralambha prema.*

bāhire viṣa-jvālā haya bhitare ānanda maya
kṛṣṇa-premera adbhūta carita

"This is the wonderful characteristic of love in separation from Kṛṣṇa: that outwardly it appears like poisonous burning, but inwardly it tastes like nectarean ecstasy."

—*Caitanya-caritāmṛta, Madhya* 28.271

In this concluding verse Mahāprabhu revealed His heart to Kṛṣṇa in the most exalted love-dedicating mood of the Vraja *gopīs*.

āśliṣya vā pāda-ratāṁ pinaṣṭu mām
adarśanān-marma-hatāṁ karotu vā
yathā tathā vā vidadhātu lampaṭo
mat-prāṇa-nāthas-tu sa eva nāparaḥ

"Kṛṣṇa may embrace Me in love or trample Me under His feet. He may break My heart by hiding Himself from Me. Let that libidinous monarch do whatever He likes, but He will always be the only Lord of My life."

Śrīla Guru Mahārāja explained that the *gopīs* experienced the most unprecedented and extraordinary type of love-attraction to Kṛṣṇa which never faded, no matter how He treated them. Their quality of exclusive and unconditional devotion has been revealed through this verse. Pointing out the glory of such incomparable *gopī prema*, Śrīla Guru Mahārāja commented: "*Vraja-rasa-lampaṭasya svairācāreṣ ātma-nikṣepasyaiva paramotkarṣaḥ*—The acme of self-dedication is to unconditionally surrender to the whim of Śrī Kṛṣṇa, the autocratic paramour of Vṛndāvana."

—*Prapanna-jīvanāmṛta* 7.22

Remembering Mahāprabhu with tears of gratitude, Śrīla Guru Mahārāja deeply adored such self-surrender and aspired for such great fortune with ceaseless thirst. He often loved to sing to himself a few lines from one of Ṭhākura Bhaktivinoda's songs which expressed these sublime feelings of pure self-surrender.

yāhe tāra sukha haya sei sukha mama
nija sukhe-duḥkhe mora sarvadāi sama

bhakativinoda saṁyoge viyoge
tāhe jāne prāṇeśvara
tāra sukhe sukhī sei prāṇa-nātha
se kabhu nā haya para

"Whichever way He feels satisfied to treat me is my happiness. I will receive pleasure and pain, happiness and sorrow equally for His cause. Whether in union or separation, Bhaktivinoda always knows Him as none other than the supreme beloved Lord of his life."

—*Gītāvalī, Śikṣāṣṭaka* 8

Chapter Five

ŚRĪ RĀDHĀ-TATTVA

Śrīla Guru Mahārāja beautifully described the unique position of Śrī Rādhikā as the supreme consort of Kṛṣṇa, the beautiful Divine Goddess and Supreme Female Personality of the Absolute Truth. She is simultaneously different and nondifferent from Śrī Kṛṣṇa. This inconceivable eternal principle was revealed by Śrī Caitanya Mahāprabhu as the *acintya bheda-abheda siddhānta.*

While Śrī Kṛṣṇa is *pūrṇa śaktimān,* the self-perfect original enjoyer of all universal power and pleasure, Śrī Rādhā is His *pūrṇa śakti,* the unlimited power and universal pleasure potency itself;

While He is omnipotent, She is the omnipotency;

While He is the subject, She is His object;

While He is beautiful, She is beauty;

While He is supreme ecstatic pleasure, She is the pleasure potency and unlimited relisher of that pleasure;

While He is the supreme enjoyer, She is the enjoyment potency and the supremely enjoyed;

While He is supremely worshipable, She is the supreme principle of all worship and the supreme worshiper;

While He is supremely lovable, She is the supreme love and lover;

And while He is the supreme object of devotion, She is the supreme principle of devotion and supreme relisher of that devotional ecstasy.

In this way, by Her unlimited attributes Śrī Rādhikā is known as Śrī Kṛṣṇa's 'separate second self' and the only sustaining counterpart that ever, vitalizes the ecstatic love dalliance of the *ādi puruṣa* Śrī Govinda.

This eternal Śrī Rādhā-*tattva* was first manifest on the earthly plane through a few condensed but brief descriptions found in the *Śrutis* and Purāṇas. The *Brahma-vaivarta Purāṇa* contains the most unique and extensive descriptions, while some equally esoteric but more mysterious descriptions are found in the *Bhāgavata Purāṇa* (*Śrīmad Bhāgavatam*).

anayārādhito nūnaṁ
bhagavān harir-īśvaraḥ
yan no vihāya govindaḥ
prīto yām anayad rahaḥ
—*Śrīmad Bhāgavatam* 10.30.28

This *śloka* describes how, during His joyful love-pastimes with all the beautiful damsels of Vraja, Kṛṣṇa specifically took one of them to a secluded bower, recognizing Her superlative devotion as the best of all. Exalted pure devotees have realized the significance of this *līlā* and have revealed that the damsel taken by Kṛṣṇa was none other than Śrī Rādhikā. They explained that the term '*ārādhito*' is the mystic confidential reference to the name 'Rādhā' (the personification of devotion). This verse was spoken by the *gopīs* who were left behind. Understanding that their principal and peerless goddess had enchanted Him the most, they glorified Śrī Rādhikā, their most fortunate friend, saying that Her adoration of Govinda had excelled theirs. Therefore He had chosen Her exclusively, leaving all others behind and had taken Her to a lonely spot to have more intimate pastimes in Her company.

In this connection Śrīla Guru Mahārāja has beautifully presented the essence of this *siddhānta* in his own language and realization:

yadamiya-mahimā-śrī-bhāgavatyāṁ kathāyāṁ
pratipadam anubhūtam apyālabdhā-abhidheyā
tadakhila-rasa-mūrteḥ śyāma-līlāvalamvaṁ
madhura-rasadhī-rādhā-pāda padmaṁ prapadye

"It is She, Śrī Rādhā, whose unlimited nectarean glories, qualities, beauty, and love for Kṛṣṇa have always been deeply felt and recognized throughout the entire *Bhāgavatam* at every step of the ultimate meaning and purport of all its descriptions. Yet out of feelings of great reverence and with the pure intention to protect Her exalted honour from certain neophyte devotees present in that open assembly, Her name was not directly mentioned by Śrīla Śukadeva Goswāmī. She therefore remains mysteriously hidden as the most confidential ultimate objective of life. She is the shelter and promoter of all divine pastimes of Kṛṣṇa, who is the personification of all beauty and bliss. I offer my most regardful obeisances unto the lotus feet of Śrī Rādhikā, who is the unlimited ocean of all the conjugal love-mellows of Kṛṣṇa."

Within more recent history, Śrī Rādhikā's *aprākṛta-līlā* (transcendental pastimes) became first manifest in the spontaneous devotional realization of great devotees such as Jayadeva Goswāmī, Candidāsa, Vidyāpati, and then ultimately through the transcendental life and precepts of Śrī Caitanya Mahāprabhu, who is realized by His devotees as the full-bloomed personification of Her *mahābhāva*. He was adored by the devotees as *rādhā-bhāva-dyuti suvalita*—Kṛṣṇa Himself, fully imbued and beautified with Her divine love and complexion. Mahāprabhu revealed to the world the incomparable glory and unique position of Śrī Rādhikā, the abode of Kṛṣṇa-*prema*. The following verse describes that invaluable contribution:

yadi gaura nā haita tabe ki haita kemone dharitāma e de
rādhāra mahimā prema-rasa-sīmā jagate jānāta ke
madhura vṛndā-vipina mādhurī-praveśa-cāturī-sāra
varaja yuvatī bhāvera bhakati śakati haita kāra

"What great insurmountable, unsurpassable loss would we have faced in our life if Śrī Gaurāṅga had not appeared before us on this Earth? How could we bear our unfulfilled, empty lives without Him? Who in this world would have described the superexcellent transcendental glory of Śrī Rādhikā, who is the last limit of divine love and devotion for the Supreme Lord Kṛṣṇa? Without His grace, who would be able to know the excellent devotional path that gives entrance into the transcendental realm of the ambrosial ecstasy of Vṛndāvana? Who would be able to attain the mood and taste of the topmost devotional ecstasy of the young damsels of Vraja?"

—*Vāsu Ghoṣa/ Narahari Sarakāra*

premā nāmādbhutārthaḥ śravaṇa-patha-gataḥ kasya nāmnāṁ mahimnaḥ
ko vettā kasya vṛndāvana-vipina-mahā-mādhurīṣu praveśaḥ
ko vā jānāti rādhāṁ parama-rasa-camatkāra-mādhurya-sīmāṁ
ekaś-caitanya-candraḥ parama-karuṇayā sarvam āviścakāra

"Who would have been so fortunate to imbibe the ambrosial meaning of '*prema*,' the wonderful ecstasy of love for Kṛṣṇa, within the core of their heart through the pathway of their ears? Who would have truly known the inner mean-

ing of the divine Holy Names? Who would have discovered entrance into the innermost sweet love-pastimes of Vṛndāvana? Who would have properly understood Śrī Rādhā-*tattva* as the last limit of infinite love-ecstasy? It is only Śrī Caitanyacandra who has mercifully revealed all this."
—Śrīla Prabodhānanda Saraswatī, *Caitanya-candrāmṛta, v.*130

Śrīla Guru Mahārāja deeply understood the transcendental characteristics of Śrī Caitanya Mahāprabhu as the living personification of Śrī Rādhā-*prema*. He felt great love for Śrī Rādhikā promoted by his profound loving devotion to Śrīmān Mahāprabhu, and he simultaneously felt intense devotional love for Śrīmān Mahāprabhu through his love of Śrī Rādhikā. Rādhā-*tattva* is actually nondifferent from Kṛṣṇa-*tattva*, but in order to relish the nectarean *līlā* of union with each other, They divided into two: Rasarāja and Mahābhāva. Rasarāja is all ecstasy and beauty personified, the enjoyer of His own ecstatic self and the supremely cherished object of all love. Mahābhāva is the personification of this nectarean love for Rasarāja. He receives ecstasy by enjoying Her, and She loves to be enjoyed by Him (predominating and predominated moieties). Thus, because of Her inseparable, intimate relation to Kṛṣṇa, Śrī Rādhikā is defined as simultaneously distinct and non-distinct from Him.

rādhā pūrṇa-śakti, kṛṣṇa pūrṇa-śaktimāna
dui vastu bheda nāhi, śāstra-paramāṇa
mṛgamada, tāra gandha yaiche aviccheda
agni, jvālāte yaiche kabhu nāhi bheda
rādhā-kṛṣṇa aiche sadā eka-i svarūpa
līlā-rasa āsvādite dhare dui-rūpa

"Śrī Rādhā is the perfectly complete Power, and Lord

Kṛṣṇa is the possessor of that divine Power. As revealed by the holy scriptures, They are nondifferent, just as musk and its fragrance or fire and its heat are inseparable. Śrīmatī Rādhārāṇī and Śrī Kṛṣṇa are indeed one, yet They have assumed two forms in order to relish the nectar of Their *līlā*."

—*Śrī Caitanya-caritāmrta, Ādi* 4.96-98

One of the great contributions that Śrīla Guru Mahārāja himself made to the world of Rādhā-*dāsyam* was his commentary on the *Brahma-gāyatrī*. He had the revelation within his heart that the deepest and ultimate meaning of *Śrī Brahma-gāyatrī* was Rādhā-*dāsyam*. He composed his *Gāyatrī-bhāṣya*, which is one of his greatest works and an unparalleled beacon-light of Gauḍīya *siddhānta*.

bhvādes tat savitur vareṇya-vihitaṁ kṣetra-jña sevyārthakaṁ
bhargo vai vṛṣabhānuj-ātma-vibhavaikārādhanā-śrī-puram
bhargo jyotir-acintya-līlana-sudhaikārādhanā-śrī-puram
bhargo dhāma-taraṅga khelana sudhaikārādhanā-śrī-puram
bhargo dhāma sadā-nirasta-kuhakaṁ prajñāna-līlā-puram

devasyāmṛta-rūpa-līla-rasadher-ārādha-dhīḥ preriṇaḥ
devasyāmṛta-rūpa-līla-puruṣasyārādha-dhīḥ preṣiṇaḥ
devasya dyuti-sundaraika-puruṣasyārādhya-dhīḥ preṣiṇaḥ

gāyatrī-muralīṣṭa-kīrtana-dhanaṁ rādhā-padaṁ dhīmahi
gāyatrī-gaditaṁ mahāprabhu-mataṁ rādhā-padaṁ dhīmahi
dhīr-ārādhanam eva nānyad-iti tad-rādhā-padaṁ dhīmahi

"With all of your thoughts and heart's desire, fully engage yourself in the pure devotional service and worship of *bhargo*, the Supreme Goddess Śrī Rādhikā, who is the unlimited origin and possessor of the *svarūpa-śakti* of Kṛṣṇa, the Supreme Beautiful Godhead (*deva*). Being the ultimate and all-harmonizing potency of Kṛṣṇa, She remains His eternally unexcelled beloved servitor. In order to fully enrich and promote His *līlā-vilāsa,* She manifests Herself in variegated congenial forms. It is She who manifests Herself as Goloka-*dhāma,* the abode of Kṛṣṇa, in the form of beautiful effulgence (*saundarya-jyoti*) and opulence (*vaibhava*), adorning and glorifying Him all around. It is She who extends Herself as Līlā-śakti, the potency principle which promotes the bliss-giving pastimes of Śrī Kṛṣṇa in variegated, colorful, tasteful, mystically opulent and beautiful ways. She is the unlimited ocean of love of Kṛṣṇa personified (*mahābhāva svarūpinī*). Therefore adore Her as the supreme goal of life who gives venerable, blessed intelligence, realization, and taste of enhanced loving worship toward Her and Her eternal beloved *deva,* Śrī Kṛṣṇa, the all-perfect fulfillment of life."

Śrīla Guru Mahārāja further blessed us with the most significant and confidential meaning of *Brahma-gāyatrī,* the song of pure liberation, by revealing the conclusive commentary which manifested from a beautiful revelation in his loving heart. It is the very nature of this divine vibration to ultimately connect us to Lord Kṛṣṇa's flute-song, which is none other than the pure love song from the heart of the *mantram.* This flute-song is naturally full of Rādhā-*prema* and is dedicated to giving pleasure to Her.

What is the special function of this all-attractive flute-song in the lives of devoted aspirants? That it deeply attracts the entirety of their souls to the unending beauty, glory, and qualities of Kṛṣṇa's eternal beloved, Śrīmatī Rādhārāṇī, and properly settles them in their own respective positions in Her eternal, ecstatic service. In other words, on the higher level of *Gāyatrī-sādhanā,* Kṛṣṇa's flute-song deeply inspires the devotees to embrace the identity of an artist-servitor in the divine concert-performance of His eternal consort Śrī Rādhā's loving service through harmonious participation.

Thus, the innermost direction of this flute-song is *Rādhā-padam dhīmahi*—"By all means, wholeheartedly embrace the service to the lotus feet of My beloved consort Śrīmatī Rādhārānī with all devotional love." The highest and innermost teachings of Śrīman Mahāprabhu are fully represented in this one line "*Rādhā-padam dhīmahi,*" which is *Gāyatrī-nigudārtha,* the confidential nectar-essence of the *Gāyatrī mantram.* Therefore the ultimate objective of all pure devotional worship performed in the lives of the fortunately intelligent persons is none other than this—"*Rādhā-padam dhīmahi.*"

The culmination of Śrīla Guru Mahārāja's lifetime of devotion to the service of Śrī Rādhikā was the full-fledged fortune of understanding Her *tattva.* As a most humble follower and servitor, he vividly traced out the current of *rāgātmikā prema* as it flowed from the grace of his *gurudeva* Śrīla Saraswatī Ṭhākura and other *guru-varga,* ornamented as it was by their esoteric contributions. Being identified with them, his esoteric self became imbued with Rādhikā-*prema* and he thereby profoundly dedicated himself to Her pure devotional service. With a guardian's care and affection, he taught how to approach Rādhā-*tattva* with all reverence and adoration, and he presented so much valuable heart-attracting information about Her. Glorifying his worshipable goddess in loving devotion was the great happiness of Śrīla Guru Mahārāja's heart, and thus he was found to frequently utter the following song composed by Śrīla Rūpa Goswāmī. Enchanted by the ambrosial loveliness of Śrī Rādhikā, Śrīla Rūpa Goswāmī felt deeply inspired to glorify his beloved Goddess with intimate devotion.

rādhe jaya jaya mādhava-dayite
gokula-taruṇī-maṇḍala-mahīte

dāmodara-rati-vardhana-veśe
hari-niṣkuṭa-vṛndā-vipineśe

vṛṣabhānu dadhi-nava-śaśī lekhe
lalitā-sakhī-guṇa-ramita-viśākhe

karuṇāṁ kuru-mayi karuṇā-bharite
sanaka-sanātana-varnita-carite

"O Rādhe, Your transcendental love and beauty are so powerful and attractive that they captivate even the heart of Mādhava, who is eternally self-fulfilled as the unlimited source of all divine ecstasy and charm. By Your own natural excellence You are the most adorable of all of the young beautiful damsels of Gokula-maṇḍala, and therefore Your glories remain perpetually unequaled.

"O Rādhe, Your elegant countenance, decorated by coquettish moods and captivating dress, ever increase the love-ecstasy of Your beloved Dāmodara. Manifesting such unique loveliness, You forever remain the beloved queen of the beautiful forest groves of Hari, who is expert in stealing away Your heart by creating an irresistible love-attraction.

"O Rādhe, from the ocean of Vṛṣabhānu, You have risen like a full moon of exquisite beauty that ever delights the heart of Mādhava. You are very fond of Lalitā and Viśākhā, who stand out amongst all the other damsels of Gokula due to their charming beauty and expertise in *prema-sevā*. They are also deeply captivated and overwhelmed by Your super-excellent qualities which enchant Kṛṣṇa, the divine monarch of all loving mellows, and so they accept You with all adoration as their beloved Goddess and exclusive shelter of their lives.

"O Rādhe, Your transcendental glories are described with unending joy by the exalted saints like Sanaka Ṛṣi and Your intimate servitor Śrīla Sanātana Goswāmī. O magnanimous Goddess! Your heart is full of compassion; therefore, please bestow Your mercy upon me."

Being so appreciative of this divine fortune in his life, Śrīla Guru Mahārāja could not bear the fact that anyone would worship Śrī Kṛṣṇa without Śrī Rādhikā or dishonor Her in any way. By reciting the following song by Śrīla Bhaktivinoda Ṭhākura, he reaffirmed the fact that worship of Śrī Kṛṣṇa which was devoid of sincere reverence for Śrīmati Rādhārānī would ultimately become null and void.

rādhā-bhajane yadi mati nāhi bhelā
kṛṣṇa-bhajana tava akāraṇa gelā

ātapa-rahita sūraya nāhi jāni
rādhā-virahita mādhava nāhi māni

kevala mādhava pūjaye sa ajñānī
rādhā anādara karai abhimānī

kavahi nāhi karavi tākara saṅga
citte icchasi yadi vraja-rasa-raṅga

rādhikā-dāsī yadi haya abhimān
śīghra-i mila-i tava gokula-kān

brahmā śiva nārada śruti nārāyaṇī
rādhikā-pada-raja pūjaye māni

umā ramā satyā śacī candrā rukmiṇī
rādhā-avatāra sabe āmnāya-vāṇī

hena rādhā-paricaryā yākara dhana
bhakativinoda tāra māgaye caraṇa

"If your desire to worship Śrī Rādhā is not awakened, your worship of Kṛṣṇa will have very little benefit. Just as the sun is not perceived without sunlight, similarly I cannot accept Mādhava without Śrī Rādhikā. One who worships Kṛṣṇa alone has imperfect knowledge, and one who disrespects Śrī Rādhikā is simply conceited and full of vanity. Never associate with such a person if you at all desire the transcendentally delightful pastimes of Vraja to appear within your heart. If you consider yourself to be a maidservant of Śrī Rādhikā, then you will very soon meet Kāna (Kṛṣṇa), the Lord of Gokula. Even Lord Brahmā, Lord Śiva, Devarṣi Nārada, the personified Vedas (*Śrutis*), and Lakṣmīdevī honor and worship the dust of Śrī Rādhikā's lotus feet. The Vedic scriptures (*amnāya*) declare that Umā, Ramādevī, Satyabhāmā, Indra's wife Śacī, Candrāvalī, and Rukmiṇī are all the expansions of Śrīmatī Rādhārāṇī. Bhaktivinoda, whose only wealth is the service of Śrī Rādhā Ṭhākurāṇī, humbly begs the shelter of Her lotus feet."

—Ṭhākura Bhaktivinoda, *Gītāvalī*

Like Ṭhākura Bhaktivinoda, Śrīla Saraswatī Ṭhākura, and other Svarūpa-Rūpa-Raghunāthānuga *guru-varga*, Śrīla Guru Mahārāja also embraced the exclusive and unalloyed path of Śrī Rādhikā *prema-sevā* (*rādhā-kaiṅkarya*). The other songs by Śrīla Bhaktivinoda Ṭhākura in regard to Śrī Rādhikā such as *Rādhikā caraṇa-padma, Virajāra pāre śuddha, Ramaṇī śiromaṇi, Rasika nāgarī gaṇa śiromaṇi, Mahābhāva cintāmaṇi, Śata koṭī gopī mādhava mana*; and the descriptions of Śrī Rādhikā from the Goswāmīs' writings such as *Bhakti-rasāmṛta-sindhu, Ujjvala-nīlamaṇi, Lalita-mādhava, Vidagdha-mādhava, Utkalikā-vallarī, Stavamālā, Haṁsadūta, Uddhava-sandeśa, Gopāla-campu, Śrī Rādhā-rasa-sudhā-nidhi, Saṅgīta-mādhava, Vilāpa-kusumāñjalī, Govinda-līlāmṛta, Caitanya-caritāmṛta, Kṛṣṇa-bhāvanāmṛta,* and various *Rādhikā-aṣṭakams* were all very dear to his heart.

Śrīla Guru Mahārāja would fondly relish verses in relation to Śrī Rādhikā wherever they were to be found. Verses such as *Priyaḥ so'yam, Kiṁ pādānte, Rādhe vṛndāvanādhīśe, Govinda-ballabhe rādhe, Mahābhāva-svarūpatvam,* and *Devī kṛṣṇa-mayī-proktā,* etc. would all deeply inspire him. Besides the writings of the Goswāmīs he also felt great satisfaction of heart being absorbed in the padavali songs of Jayadeva, Vidyāpati, Caṇḍidāsa, Rāya Rāmānanda, Jñāna dāsa, and Govinda dāsa, some of which follow:

rūpa lāgi āṅkhi jhure guṇe mana bhora
prati aṅga lāgi kānde prati aṅga mora
hiyāra paraśa lāgi hiyā mora kānde
parāṇa pīriti lāgi thira nāhi bāndhe

"(Śrī Rādhā said:) Seeing the festival of His divine beauty, My eyes shed tears, My intoxicated mind is fully absorbed in tasting His virtues, every part of Me deeply craves for every part of Him, and My heart incessantly yearns for the thrill of His touch. O *sakhī*, by such intense, irresistible love-attraction, My heart cannot wait to embrace Him."

—Jñāna dāsa

sai kevā śunāila śyāma nāma
kāṇera bhitare diyā marame paśila go
ākula karila mora prāṇa

nā jāni kateka madhu śyāma nāme āche go
badana chāḍite nāhi pāre
japite japite nāma abaśa karila go
kemane pāiba sai tāre
nāma paratāpe yāra aichana karila go
aṅgera paraśe kibā haya
yekhāne basati tāra nayane heriyā go
dharama-karama kaiche raya
pāsarite kari mane pāsarā nā yāya go
ki kariba ki habe upāya
kahe dvija caṇḍīdāse kulavatī kula nāśe
āpanāra sarvasva (yauvana) yācāya

"O dear friend, that person who let me hear the name Śyāma was indeed a great friend of mine. Through my ears, that Name entered the core of my heart, deeply captivated my mind, and overwhelmed me with deep ecstatic love. As I say that nectarean Name, I cannot fathom the depth of its ambrosial sweetness. My mouth cannot give up repeatedly tasting it due to the unprecedented wonderful attachment that floods my whole existence. By constant remembrance and contemplation on that beloved Śyāma-*nāma*, my body, mind, and heart have all become charmed and stunned with love. O dear friend, I cannot wait any longer; please advise me—how can I have Him intimately in my life?

"If by merely by remembering His name I am so helpless and overwhelmed, then what astounding ambrosial experience will happen if He touches me? How can anyone go on with the ordinary affairs of life after seeing His divine form or the beauty of His abode? O my sympathetic friend, I can no longer bear my painful feelings of separation from Him, and I can no longer bear my ever-increasing thirst for His association. Therefore, I truly wish to forget all about Him so that I can get back to my normal, peaceful state of mind, but I also see to my astonishment that I am not *able* to forget Him! I am completely helpless, so please advise me: What shall I *do*? Dvija Caṇḍīdāsa, a devoted servitor of Śrī Rādhā-Śyāma, says, 'Yes! This is the way of transcendental Śyāma-*prema*! Its power releases a respectable housewife from all the moral bindings of a conservative, aristocratic society, and makes her helplessly give everything to Him!' "

—Caṇḍīdāsa

gharera bāhire daṇḍe śatabāra
tile tile uṭhe base
elāiyā veṇī bakṣa pare ṭāni
kabhu kānde kabhu hāse

"Śrī Rādhikā can no longer patiently stay in Her gorgeously opulent palace, which has become like a desolate prison to Her. In great anticipation She paces in and out of Her room, again and again looking down the path with intense longing to just catch a momentary glimpse of Kṛṣṇa. With surging desire and devotional attraction to be with Her beloved, She sometimes sits, sometimes stands, and sometimes gazes outside while absentmindedly playing with Her hair. In delightful hope and despair She first laughs, then cries...in utter restlessness."

—Caṇḍīdāsa

These songs describe Śrī Rādhikā's *pūrva-rāga-daśā,* the first awakenment of Her intense devotional love for Kṛṣṇa. Śrīla Guru Mahārāja's heart was taken away by this unparalleled exquisite taste. His inner self awakened on the plane of transcendence, incited by the incomparable, wonderful touch and taste of Śrī Rādhikā's divine love. Her restlessness and intense impatience to be with Kṛṣṇa, Her endless longing for having even a glimpse of Him, Her experience of intense love-ecstasy simply upon hearing the name of Kṛṣṇa, or Her mere thought of having His intimate company attracted his heart so profoundly that he often became overcome with devotional ecstasy. As his devotion towards Her became more intensified and developed with unique excellence, it aroused in him an endless thirst for having Her nectarean grace all through his life.

Śrīla Guru Mahārāja explained that the following song depicts Swāminī Śrī Rādhikā's *vipralambha-daśā* during the last days of Her manifest *bhauma-līlā*. The beautiful description of Śrī Rādhikā's pain of intense love in separation from Her worshipable beloved comes from the author's subjective realization. It was not an actual historic occurrence within the mundane plane of existence, because even though it apparently took place on the Earth, the *līlā* of the Divine Couple is always transcendental. The devotee enters this dimension through divine meditation and describes his revelation. The conception of laying Śrī Rādhikā's form on the lap of a desire tree which embraces Her divine body, the acute pain of sadness caused by feelings of separation, and the scene of the pastime are all transcendental to worldly happenings, even though they have been described by the devoted writer utilizing human language and concepts.

nā poḍāio rādhā-aṅga nā bhāsāio jale
marile tuliye rekho tamāleri ḍāle
āmi tamāla baḍa bhālabāsi
kṛṣṇa kāla tamāla kāla tāite
tamāla baḍa bhālabāsi
marile tuliye rekho tamāleri ḍāle

"At the acme of pain in separation from Kṛṣṇa, Śrī Rādhikā remembered the blissful intimate moments which She spent under the beautiful *tamāla* trees with Her adorable beloved. In Her divine vision imbued with those nectarean memories, She accepted the *tamāla* tree as a nondifferent expansion of Kṛṣṇa, and therefore after Her departure She wanted Her form to remain embracing this *tamāla kalpa-taru*. Expressing one of Her last desires, She said to Her *sakhīs*: 'My dearest friends, soon I will die, but please do not put My body on a funeral pyre or in the river. Just lay it on the spreading boughs of a *tamāla* tree, whom I love because he is just like My beloved.' "

—Caṇḍīdāsa

Śrīla Guru Mahārāja further explained that Śrī Rādhikā played a sweetly sad, tragic role of separation from Her beloved Kṛṣṇa similar to that found in noble romantic human love. She naturally did not have a material body to leave behind after death because She manifests Herself by Her own divine will, and therefore Her 'birth' and 'death' are only apparent. This *līlā* is considered to be a drama that enhances Śrī Rādhā's specific taste of relating to Her beloved. It was actually by the design of Rasarāja Kṛṣṇa that Rādhikā played this role, which created the scope for Him to deeply relish the love of His eternal consort in the sweet mellows of separation. Thus He aroused in Her such an endless, indescribable, intense, devotional love-hankering for His intimate association that She felt She would die from longing for His ambrosial company.

Śrīla Guru Mahārāja was fond of offering obeisances to Śrī Rādhikā with another verse composed by Śrīla Prabodhānanda Saraswatī, which was also a favorite of his Guru Mahārāja, Śrīla Saraswatī Ṭhākura.

yasyā kadāpi vasanāñcala khelanottha
dhanyāti-dhanya pavanena kṛtārtha mānī
yogīndra durgama gatiḥ madhusūdano'pi
tasyā namo'stu vṛṣabhānu bhuvo diśe'pi

"From a reverential distance, with all adoration I offer my obeisances unto the daughter of King Vṛṣabhānu, Śrī Rādhikā, who captivated the heart of Kṛṣṇa, the Supreme Lord, who is rarely attained even by the foremost of *yogīs*. Once, a gentle gust of wind wafted the sweet scent of Her clothing towards Kṛṣṇa, and He felt so blessedly fulfilled that He embraced that fragrance to His heart."

—*Rādhā-rasa-sudhā-nidhi, Maṅgalācaraṇa v.* 2

Śrīla Guru Mahārāja often prayed to Swāminī Rādhikā with tears of love in his eyes, singing a verse by Śrīla Raghunātha Dāsa Goswāmipāda from his *Vilāpa-kusumāñjalī*:

āśā-bharair-amṛta-sindhu-mayaiḥ kathañcit
kālo mayāti-gamitaḥ kila sāmpratarṁ hi
tvaṁ cet kṛpāṁ mayi vidhāsyasi naiva kiṁ me
prāṇair-vrajena ca varoru bakāriṇāpi

"O Varoru, my beautiful, most magnanimous Goddess, my heart is flooded with an ocean of nectarean hopes. I have somehow been passing my time until now eagerly longing for Your grace, which is an ocean of ever-cherished nectar. If still You do not bestow Your mercy upon me, then of what use to me are my life, the land of Vraja, or even Śrī Kṛṣṇa, who without You is simply a mighty hero who destroyed the demoniac forces like Bakāsura."

—*Vilāpa Kusumāñjalī* 102

Thus situated in the exalted world of dedication to Swāminī Rādhikā, Śrīla Guru Mahārāja continued his endless craving for Her grace, the unending ocean of all-fulfilling nectar. Journeying through the path of ambrosial realization, he came to the conclusion that the original and highest manifestation of Kṛṣṇa as *aprākṛta navīna madana* is only available when He is with Śrī Rādhikā, and the topmost ecstasy of Kṛṣṇa-*prema* can only be attained through Rādhā-*kaiṅkarya* in the mood and form of a damsel of Goloka.

Chapter Six

MAÑJARĪ-TATTVA

śrī caitanya mano'bhīṣṭaṁ
sthāpitaṁ yena bhūtale
svayaṁ rūpa kadā mahyaṁ
dadāti sva-padāntikaṁ

"O, when will Śrīla Rūpa Goswāmī, who has firmly established in this world the pure devotional teachings and principles of Śrī Caitanya Mahāprabhu and thus fulfilled His cherished desires, ever bless me with the eternal shelter of his lotus feet?"

—Narottama dāsa Ṭhākura

Śrīla Guru Mahārāja composed a *praṇāma mantra* in glorification of Śrīla Rūpa Goswāmī in the *maṅgalācaraṇa* of his presentation of *Bhakti-rasāmṛta-sindhu* as follows:

śrī-caitanya-dayā-sudhā-dhuni-dharo-dāmodar-āmodado
rāmānanda-sanātanānuga-raghu-śrī-jīva-jīvya-prabhuḥ
rādhā-śyāma-rasāmṛtābdhi-makara-brātaika-samrāḍ-hi yaḥ
sa śrī-rūpa ihāmṛtābdhi-laharī-sparśe spṛhāṁ yacchatu

"With innermost hankering, I desire to embrace the waves of the ambrosial ocean known as *Bhakti-rasāmṛta-sindhu* manifested by Śrīla Rūpa Goswāmipāda. He is the paragon of the nectarean mercy of Śrī Caitanya Mahāprabhu and he enchants Śrīla Svarūpa Dāmodara by his beautiful qualities. He is the loving follower of Śrī Rāmānanda Rāya and Sanātana Goswāmipāda, and is as dear as life to Śrī Raghunātha Dāsa Goswāmī and Śrī Jīva Goswāmī. He is the foremost 'kingfish' in the nectarean ocean of ecstatic divine love of Rādhā-Śyāma."

Śrīla Rūpa Goswāmī was one of the foremost beloved associates of Śrī Caitanya Mahāprabhu. His love and devotion for both Mahāprabhu and the Divine Couple were known to be extraordinary. Śrī Caitanya Mahāprabhu especially empowered him to reveal to the world the highest conception of devotional service to Śrī Śrī Rādhā-Kṛṣṇa, and Śrīla Guru Mahārāja was especially fond of the following presentations about him.

kṛṣṇa-tattva-bhakti-tattva-rasa-tattva-prānta
saba śikhāila prabhu bhāgavata-siddhānta

Śrī Caitanya Mahāprabhu taught Śrīla Rūpa Goswāmī the ultimate conclusions of *Śrīmad Bhāgavatam*: the truth about Lord Kṛṣṇa, devotional service, and transcendental mellows, culminating in conjugal love between Rādhā and Kṛṣṇa."

—*Śrī Caitanya-caritāmṛta, Madhya* 19.115

śrī-rūpa-hṛdaye prabhu śakti sañcārilā
sarva-tattva-nirūpaṇe 'pravīṇa' karilā

"In this way, by infusing the heart of Śrīla Rūpa Goswāmī with special potency, Śrī Caitanya Mahāprabhu empowered him to ascertain and define the conclusions of all divine truths."

—*Śrī Caitanya-caritāmṛta, Madhya* 19.117

Śrīla Guru Mahārāja explained how the unique qualities, devotional taste, and realization of Śrīla Rūpa Goswāmī became more and more obvious to the foremost associates of Mahāprabhu, who recognized the symptoms of his exalted level of consciousness and thus could not but feel profound appreciation for him. Śrīmān Mahāprabhu Himself also became deeply enchanted by Śrī Rūpa's excellent understanding of the deepest esoteric truths of ecstatic love. This was proven when Mahāprabhu recited the verse *'yaḥ kaumārah'* before the chariot of Lord Jagannātha. This was considered an ordinary mundane verse from the *Kāvya-prakāśa*, and as such, some of the devotees could not clearly understand why Mahāprabhu was reciting it. However, Śrīla Svarūpa Dāmodara Goswāmī and Śrīla Rūpa Goswāmī fully understood Mahāprabhu's inner mood. Feeling deep inspiration, Śrīla Rūpa Goswāmī then composed his famous Sanskrit verse *'priyaḥ so'yam kṛṣṇa'* explaining the intimate purport to the mood of Mahāprabhu. Eventually when Mahāprabhu discovered the verse inscribed on a palm leaf hidden in the roof of Śrī Rūpa's thatched hut, He became charmed by the fine quality of his realization and extraordinary ability to understand His mind. He fondly patted Rūpa with profound feelings of appreciation and asked Śrīla Svarūpa Dāmodara Goswāmī, "How did Rūpa know My heart?" To which Svarūpa pleasantly replied, "Prabhu, such ability in Śrī Rūpa is definite proof of Your empowerment and special grace upon him."

Thus suffused with the grace of Mahāprabhu, whom he accepted in his heart as the unified manifestation of the Divine Couple, Śrīla Rūpa Goswāmī revealed the most authentic, authoritative, and elegant devotional literature describing the transcendental nature, conclusions, and intimate pastimes of Śrī Rādhā and Kṛṣṇa. Being imbued with the beauty of this deep devotional realization, his famously-known writings and compositions such as *Śrī-Bhakti-rasāmṛta-sindhu, Ujjvala-nīlamaṇi, Lalita-mādhava, Vidagdha-mādhava, Śrī Upadeśāmṛtam, Danā-keli-kaumudī, Laghu-Bhāgavatamṛtam, Utkalikā-vallarī, Stavamālā,* and *Padyāvalī* came to be considered the most valuable treasure in the world of intimate loving service to the Lord. Śrīla Guru Mahārāja composed his *Śrīmad Rūpa-pada-rajaḥ-prārthanā-daśakam* to describe and honor this exalted contribution.

gaura-deśāc-ca vṛndā-vipinam iha parikramya nīlācalaṁ yo
gatvā kāvyāmṛtaiḥ svair-vraja-yuva-yugala-krīḍanārthaiḥ prakāmam
rāmānanda-svarūpādibhir-api-kavibhis-tarpayāmāsa gauraṁ
sa śrī-rūpaḥ kadā māṁ nija-pada-rajasā-bhūṣitaṁ saṁvidhatte

"When, on the order of Lord Gaurāṅga, Śrī Rūpa visited Puruṣottama-kṣetra after completing his circumambulation of Vraja-maṇḍala, he gave great pleasure to Śrī Caitanyadeva and the sagacious assemblage of devotees headed by Śrī Svarūpa Dāmodara and Rāmānanda Rāya with his ambrosial poetry describing the pastimes of the Divine Couple of Vraja. When will that Śrīmad Rūpa Prabhu grace me with the dust of his lotus feet?"

—*Śrī Prapanna-jīvanāmṛta,*
Rūpa-pada-raja-prārthanā-daśakam 7

By establishing the pure code of conduct in devotion and revealing the beautiful path of *rāga-mārga,* Śrīla Rūpa Goswāmī became more and more manifest as the self-effulgent *guru* of *rāgānuga bhakti.* Śrīla Guru Mahārāja described his special quality of *śuddha rāgānuga bhakti* in the following verse.

kaivalya-prema-bhūmāv-akhila-rasa-sudhā-sindhu-sañcāra-dakṣaṁ
jñātvāpy-evān ca rādhā-pada-bhajana-sudhāṁ līlayāpāyayad yam
śaktiṁ sañcārya gauro nija-bhajana-sudhā-dāna-dakṣaṁ cakāra
sa śrī-rūpaḥ kadā māṁ nija-pada-rajasā-bhūṣitaṁ saṁvidhatte

"Śrī Gaurahari knew that as an eternal associate of the Lord, Śrī Rūpa was already proficient in wandering throughout the ambrosial ocean of all the mellows in the land of unalloyed love (Vraja-*rasa*). Nonetheless, to expand His own pastimes, the Lord enabled him to drink the sweet ecstasy of servitude unto Śrī Rādhā and he thus empowered him with the skill to distribute the nectar of His personal devotional service. When will that Śrīmad Rūpa Prabhu grace me with the dust of his lotus feet?
—*Śrī Prapanna-jīvanāmṛta, Rūpa-pada-raja-prārthanā-daśakam* 6

Śrīla Guru Mahārāja had the subjective realization that the relationship of Mahāprabhu and Śrīla Rūpa Goswāmī showed a confidential aspect of Mahāprabhu's *līlā,* which was to reveal the *rasika* position of His intimate associates according to their respective *rasa* and constitutional nature. To unfold the transcendental pastimes of Vṛndāvana, Mahāprabhu tasted the *bhava* of Śrī Rādhikā and enabled His intimate associates to enter into their *nitya-siddha* forms in Vraja-*līlā* as *gopīs* and *mañjarīs*. Thus Śrīla Rūpa Goswāmī's identity as Śrī Rūpa Mañjarī, who is ever engaged in the intimate *rāga-sevā* of the Divine Couple as the leader of all the *mañjarīs* and the foremost representation of full- fledged *mañjarī-tattva,* became more and more revealed. Śrīla Guru Mahārāja fondly remembered Śrī Dhyānacandra Goswāmī's subjective glimpse into the personality and appearance of Śrī Rūpa Mañjarī as manifest on the transcendental plane of Goloka Vṛndāvana.

kuñjo'sti rūpollāsākhyo lalitā-kuñjakottare
sadā tiṣṭhati tatraiva suśobhā rūpa-mañjarī
priya-narma-sakhī-mukhyā sundarī-rūpa-mañjarī
gorocanā-samāṅga-śrīḥ keki-patrāṁśuka-priyā
sārdha-tridaśa-varṣāsau vāma-madhyātvam āśritā
raṅgaṇā-mālikā ceti pravadanti manīṣinaḥ
iyaṁ lavaṅga-mañjaryā ekenāhnā kanīyasī
kalau gaura-rasa-rūpa-gosvāmitvaṁ samāgata

"In the northern part of Śrī Lalitā Sakhī's *kuñja* lies Śrī Rūpollāsa-*kuñja,* where the most beautiful and attractive Śrī Rūpa Mañjarī resides. She is the foremost amongst those *gopīs* who are known as *priya-narma sakhīs* and is distinguished by her graceful, captivating countenance and unique loveliness. Her complexion is bright gold—the color of *gorocanā*—and she delights in wearing a dress adorned with the multicolors of a peacock's splendid tail-feathers. Her age is thirteen-and-a-half years, and her nature is *bāmya madhyā.* The *pandits* call her '*raṅganā-mallikā*'—a charming damsel who entertains and enchants the heart of Kṛṣṇa by her graceful dance and her jasmine-flowerlike beauty and fragrance. She is one day younger than Lavaṅga Mañjarī, and in Gaura-*līlā* she appears as Śrīla Rūpa Goswāmī. In *Kiśorī-tantra* Śrī Rūpa Mañjarī has been described by the eight-syllable *mantra Śrīṁ rūpa mañjaryai svāhā.* I offer myself in all devotion to the service of beautiful Śrī Rūpa Mañjarī, and further meditate upon her as follows:

gorocanā-nindi-nijāṅga-kāntiṁ
mayūra-piñchābha-sucina-vastrām
śrī-rādhikā-pāda-saroja-dāsīṁ
rūpākhyakāṁ mañjarikāṁ bhaje'ham

"I worship Śrī Rūpa Mañjarī, whose beautiful bodily complexion discredits the golden color of *gorocanā*. Wearing a dress made of fine cloth resembling peacock feathers which represents her colorful devotional character, she delightfully engages in the service of Śrī Rādhikā's lotus feet."

—*Dhyānacandra Paddhati* 294-297, 299

Śrīla Guru Mahārāja gave a beautiful explanation on the *siddhānta* of *mañjarī-tattva*. On the highest plane of divinity the form of a young damsel (*gopī*) is found to be most suitable and congenial to attract and reciprocate with the divine male *aprākṛta-navīna-madana* Kṛṣṇa in an intimate love-relationship (*mādhurya rasa*). A special class of these *gopīs* who eternally engage in the intimate service of Kṛṣṇa and Śrīmatī Rādhikā are referred to as *mañjarīs*. (The literal term '*mañjarī*' means a flowerbud cluster which has just begun to bloom.) This special characteristic blossoming stage of *prema-sevā* has a unique exquisite flavor known as *mañjarī bhāva*. The *mañjarīs* are the topmost intimate servitors of the Divine Couple, and therefore all of the confidential pastimes of Śrī Śrī Rādhā and Kṛṣṇa are freely accessible to them. By their constitutional nature, the *mañjarīs* are so fortunate that they can actually share the blissful intimate moments of the Divine Couple while rendering suitable *rāga-sevā* which is most pleasing to Them at that time.

Although the topmost Gauḍīya Vaiṣṇavas kept their divine inner sentiments mostly confidential, some of them revealed through their beautiful writings and highly developed personal characteristics their deep hankering and unending aspiration for serving the Divine Couple intimately as *mañjarīs*. They ultimately attained that divine revelation and discovered themselves in their own respective *svarūpa-siddha mañjarī* forms in Goloka Vṛndāvana with immense joy and supreme fulfillment. Through his sincere dedication to the service of the Divine Couple, Śrīla Guru Mahārāja could naturally feel the deeper inner current of pure *rūpānuga rāga-bhakti* in the life of Śrīla Saraswatī Ṭhākura, Bhaktivinoda Ṭhākura, and his other *guru-varga,* and discovered that deep within himself he had the same profound attraction and taste. Therefore he confidentially embraced the lofty shelter of Śrīla Rūpa Goswāmī in his eternal *svarūpa* as Śrī Rūpa Mañjarī.

Sometime before his departure from this plane, Śrīla Saraswatī Ṭhākura had read Śrīla Guru Mahārāja's Sanskrit composition *Bhaktivinoda-viraha-daśakam.* In that poem he noticed his exclusive adherence and devotion to *Śrī Rādhāpada-sevanāmṛta* following the stream of pure Rūpa-Vinoda-*rāga-bhakti.* He was deeply satisfied in heart knowing that the direction of Śrīla Guru Mahārāja's eternal divine identity was *mañjarī bhāva.* As confirmation and recognition of his heart's feeling, Śrīla Saraswatī Ṭhākura specifically chose to hear the unique song *Śrī-rūpa-mañjarī-pada* from him just prior to his disappearance, thus reassuring Śrīla Guru Mahārāja's shelter in the embrace of Śrīmatī Rūpa Mañjarī. Śrīla Guru Mahārāja, in reverential gratitude, described the occasion as follows:

līlā-saṁgopa-kāle-nirupadhi-karuṇā-kāriṇā-svāmināhaṁ
yat pādāvje'rpito yat pada-bhajanamayaṁ gāyayitvā tu gītam
yogyāyogyatva-bhāvaṁ mama khalu sakalaṁ duṣṭa-buddher agṛhṇan
sa śrī-rūpaḥ kadā māṁ nija-pada-rajasā-bhūṣitaṁ saṁvidhatte

"Just prior to the withdrawal of his manifest *līlā,* my causelessly merciful divine master Śrīla Saraswatī Ṭhākura handed me over to the holy feet of that divine personality by having me sing that glorious prayer unto his lotus feet.

Despite my lowliness, when will Śrī Rūpa Prabhu grace me with the dust of his holy lotus feet, ignoring all my disqualifications?"

—*Śrī Prapanna-jīvanāmṛta,*
Rūpa-pada-raja-prārthanā-daśakam 10

Remembering that blessed event, Śrīla Guru Mahārāja often sang the following song in very deep absorption.

śrī-rūpa-mañjarī-pada sei mora sampada,
sei mora bhajana-pūjana
sei mora prāṇa-dhana sei mora ābharaṇa,
sei mora jīvanera jīvana
sei mora rasa-nidhi sei mora vāñchā-siddhi
sei mora vedera dharama
sei vrata, sei tapaḥ sei mora mantra-japa,
sei mora dharama-karama
anukūla habe vidhi se pade haibe siddhi,
nirakhiba e dui nayane
se-rūpa mādhurī-rāśi prāṇa-kuvalaya-śaśī*
praphullita habe niśi-dine
tuyā adarśana ahi garale jārala dehi,
cira-dina tāpita jīvana
hā hā prabhu kara dayā deha more pada-chāyā
narottama laila śaraṇa

"The divine lotus feet and shelter of Śrī Rūpa Mañjarī are my ever-cherished invaluable wealth and the object of my devotional service and worship. They are the treasure of my heart that adorns my existence and they are the life of my life. They are the infinite reservoir of all transcendental mellows and the perfection that fulfills all my desires. They are the conclusion of the esoteric meaning of the Vedas for me. They are the goal of all of my vows, austerities, *mantras*, and meditation. They are the purpose of my inner divine existence and the spiritual activities of my soul. I am earnestly praying that the divine will of Providence will greatly favor me so that I may attain perfection in the pure loving service of her lotus feet. At that moment the moonlike beauty and radiance of Śrī Rūpa Mañjarī will appear before my eyes, captivating and bathing the lotus of my heart with rays of ecstasy constantly day and night. Presently, however, my heart burns, afflicted by the venomous bite of separation from such a beautiful life of fulfillment. Therefore, O my divine mistress Śrī Rūpa Mañjarī, my desperate need is for you to please shower your ambrosial mercy upon me, soothe me, and embrace me in the shade of your resplendent lotus feet. Narottama dāsa takes complete shelter of you."

—Narottama dāsa Ṭhākura, *Prārthanā-lālasā* 16

In his last years, Śrīla Guru Mahārāja became fully immersed in his own eternal serving mood. His inspiration to attain the service of Śrī Rūpa Mañjarī flowed like a river of divine consciousness. In this situation, his life transformed in accordance with his natural ascent to a higher dimension of constant loving service. He could feel the depth of devotional ecstasy of the *rūpānuga rasika bhaktas* and was absorbed in the moods of their *rāga-sevā*. Thus he was very fond of the following songs.

ei nava-dāsī bali śrī-rūpa cāhibe
hena śubha-kṣaṇa mora kata-dine habe
śīghra ajñā karibena dāsī heṭhā āya
sebāra susajja-kārya karaha tvarāya
ānandita hañā hiyā ajñā-bale
pavitra manete kārya karibe tat-kāle

sevāra sāmagrī ratna-thālāte kariyā
subāsita bāri svarṇa-jhārite pūriyā
doṅhāra sammukhe la'ye diba śīghra-gati
narottamera dasā kabe haibe e-mati

"I long for that day when, at some auspicious moment, Śrī Rūpa Mañjarī will affectionately recognize me and ask if I am the newly recruited maidservant whom she was expecting. Giving me a special privilege, she will affectionately order me: 'O devoted one, come forward and prepare everything very nicely for the Divine Couple.' Being empowered and inspired by her order, my heart will be filled with great delight and I will perform all required services with pure devotion. I will fervently wait for Yugala Kiśora's affectionate orders, and knowing Their needs, I will quickly carry to Them a jeweled tray of Their favorite paraphernalia. They will be pleased as I fill a golden goblet with aromatic tasty water and promptly place it before Them, running in delightful excitement. O compassionate Rūpa Mañjarī! When will I, Narottama, be blessed with the attainment of such ecstatic fulfillment?"

—Śrīla Narottama Ṭhākura, *Prārthanā* 18

śrī-rūpa paścāte āmi rahiba bhīta hañā
doṅhe punaḥ kahibena āma pāne cāñā
sadaya hṛdaye doṅhe kahibena hāsi
koṭhāya pāile rūpa ei naba dāsī
śrī-rūpa-mañjarī tabe doṅhā-bākya śuni
mañjuālī dila more ei dāsī āni
ati namra-citta āmi haibe jānilā
sebā-kārya diyā tabe hethāya rākhilā
hena tattva doṅhākāre sākṣāte kahiyā
narottame sebāya dibe niyukta kariyā

"I long for that priceless moment when, on the plane of transcendence, following behind Śrī Rūpa Mañjarī with all awe and reverence, I will meet the Divine Couple. They will graciously look at me and silently communicate Their deep affection to my heart. Compassionately smiling, They will ask, 'Śrī Rūpa, where did you find this beautiful new maid-servant?' Upon hearing this sweet inquiry, Śrī Rūpa Mañjarī will then address the Divine Couple, telling Them all about me: 'Feeling special care, my dear friend Mañjulālī thought this new girl would be sublimely dedicated to Your service, so she fondly brought her to me.' Thus, by her personal request and recommendation, Śrī Rūpa Mañjarī will eternally engage me in the devotional service of the Divine Couple of Vraja."

—*Prārthanā* 19

srī-rūpa-mañjarī sakhī kṛpā-dṛṣṭe cāñā
tāpi narottame siñca sevāmṛta diyā

"O Śrī Rūpa Mañjarī, intimate beloved friend of the Divine Couple! Please cast your merciful glance upon me. Please soothe this distressed Narottama by sprinkling the nectar of your devotional service upon me."

—*Prārthanā* 21, verse 5

śrī rūpa mañjarī sańge yābo kabe
rasa-sevā-śikṣā-tare
tad-anugā ho'ye rādhā-kuṇḍa taṭe
rahiba harṣitāntare

"When will that precious fortune be mine when Śrī Rūpa Mañjarī takes me with her to the banks of Śrī Rādhā-kuṇḍa, the most favorite place of Śrīmatī Rādhārāṇī? There she will give me lessons in the performance of *rasa-sevā*, making me follow her own example. Remaining under her affectionate care and guidance with all loyalty and obedience, I will thus ecstatically pass the time in her company."

—Bhaktivinoda Ṭhākura, *Gīta-mālā, Siddhi-lālasā* 4, verse 2

nirjana kuṭīre śrī rādhā-caraṇa
smaraṇe thākiba rata
śrī rūpa mañjarī dhīre dhīre āsi
kahibe āmāya kata

balibe o sakhī ki kara basiyā
dekhaha bāhire āsi
yugala milana śobhā nirupama
haibe caraṇa dāsī

"In my divine form of perfection in the transcendental abode of Goloka, I will be waiting in a solitary cottage, remaining absorbed in the blissful remembrance of Śrī Rādhā's lotus feet. After some time, I will see my adorable *rasika guru* and friend, Śrī Rūpa Mañjarī, approaching me, charmed and overwhelmed by some special joy. She will say to me with excitement, 'O dear friend, what are you doing sitting here? Come outside and see, your cherished dream has now come true. In that beautiful *kuñja* decorated with flowers, Śrī Rādhikā and Kṛṣṇa, the Divine Couple, are now having Their wonderful ecstatic pastimes. These love-sports are flooding everyone and everything with ambrosial ecstasy. Come with me; I will take you there to serve Them, and you will become an eternal maidservant of Their lotus feet.' "

—*Gīta-mālā, Siddhi-lālasā* 6, verses 1, 2

śrī rūpa mañjarī prabhṛtir sama
yugala sevāya āśa
avaśya se-rūpa sevā pābo āmi
parākāṣṭā su-viśvāśa

"I deeply aspire to perform confidential service to the Divine Couple similar to that which is rendered by Śrī Rūpa Mañjarī and her associates. I know that one day I will certainly attain that highest kind of service, for I so intensely long for it with absolute totality of faith."

—*Gīta-mālā, Siddhi-lālasā* 8, verse 3

During his last days, Śrīla Guru Mahārāja remained absorbed in these innermost moods of separation and hankering. Before the withdrawal of his manifest presence, he intimately remembered with deep gratitude how Śrīla Saraswatī Ṭhākura had mercifully blessed him by embracing him into the camp of Śrī Rūpa Mañjarī. He was eagerly awaiting return to his divine apprenticeship under this most intimate servitor of the Divine Goddess of his heart, Śrī Rādhikā, accompanied by his *guru* in the form of Nayanamaṇi Mañjarī on the plane of *nitya-līlā*, to eternally serve the Divine Couple under their gracious shelter.

Thus praying for the mercy of Ṭhākura Bhaktivinoda and Śrī Gadādhara Paṇḍit, who have always been a very special source of divine inspiration in the life of Śrīla Guru Mahārāja, the author completes this *Śrī-Bhakti-Rakṣaka-Bhajana-Mādhurī* on the auspicious day of their disappearance, 4th July 1997.